E

our

Angels

An inspired insight into the
Angelic Realm

By

Mary Jac

First published in Great Britain in August 2011
By MJB Publishing

ISBN 978–0–9569870–0-6

Cover designed by Matt Mills
www.blueicestudios.net

Printed in the UK by Bishops Printers, Walton
Road, Portsmouth, Hampshire

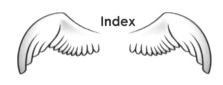

Index

For Nana, John & Luke
xxxx

Introduction

~ Where do I start? ~

I feel surrounded by angelic love wherever I am. I talk to my Angels often – ask them for help for myself and my family and friends, thank them when something good happens or they send me a sign of their presence, and reach out as if to touch them when I feel them near.

Embracing the Angels in my life has helped me with so many different things. They have given me comfort whilst grieving, reassurance during illness and guidance through the numerous signs and messages I receive in so many different ways.

The inspiration that they have given me to enable me to carry out my work with the angelic realms has enlightened and helped many other people too.

I hope that this insight into the angelic realm will comfort and inspire you, as will the additional true Angel stories from many other people, which you are sure to find both amazing and reassuring, too.

This book has been in my head and my heart for a long time and after being "nudged" by my Angels several times in recent months, I knew it was time to put pen to paper and share all the wonderful things I have seen, heard and learnt with you.

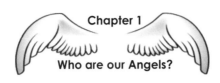

Chapter 1

Who are our Angels?

The Angel Team

Most of us know that the mighty Archangels love to be called on and that they can help thousands of people concurrently. We can also be confident that they are sure to be there for us when we need their specialist assistance – in fact you will find they are mentioned frequently here in this book.

However, the Angels who surround, help and protect us on a daily basis and assist us with all aspects of our lives, are far more personal to us – our "teams" if you like, as they all work together with us to achieve the best life possible!

Each and every one of us is unique and has our own team of Angels who love, guide and protect us through all of life's experiences.

After reading about how an Angel Team is made up, I am sure that you will know how to figure out who will be on your own ......

The Team Leader – The Guardian Angel

When we're born, we are appointed a Guardian Angel – one who stays with us at all times, coming forward to help and protect us either when called upon, or when they sense the need.

Our Guardian Angel could be a long lost ancestor, a grandparent, great grandparent or other relative. Or they may not be related to you in any way at all. They could have any name, often unusual or obscure and it may help you to discover your Guardian Angel's name by reading the 'instructions' in Chapter 8.

You might, however just prefer to give them an affectionate name or title of your own, one that suits how they appear to you in your mind's eye - especially if you have seen or had a vision of them as I have. You'll know in your heart what feels right to both you and your Angel – trust your instinct!

My Guardian Angel's name is Uriah and I have lovingly named him "my big pink fella" – you can read why in Chapter 2.

Steadfast team members

As we go through life we all sadly lose people who we are close to, and these people are then "added" to our Angel teams, as well as to the teams of their other relatives and dear ones.

I've seen it written that Angels and lost loved ones are different beings, but it's my perception that our lost loved ones are amongst our Angels and part of our teams for sure.

Their prominence or significance of role in our teams will be similar to their prominence or importance when they were part of our life on earth.

Their personalities or strengths as Angels will be no different to when they were alive. For instance, if your lost Father was a bit of a practical joker he may be playful with you now – maybe by hiding things from you in your home for a short while! Or you may have had a grandmother who was an excellent listener so there's no reason why she wouldn't want to listen to you chattering away today.

The steadfast team members will not all be with you 24/7 but will call in to visit you from time to time and will certainly be about should you need them, so talk to them whenever you want to – just as you would have done in life.

Can you visualise your team so far?

Now – through the years many different Angels will pop in and out of your life as you need them. We'll call these the "pop in" Angels.

"Pop-in" Angels
These angelic team members may be sent to you by one of the Archangels (for instance, Archangel Azrael will help you if bereaved and send you one of his trained bereavement Angels to remain by your side through the worst times for as long as you need them).

Or you may be sent an Angel to help you with a creative project, who will stay with you to see it through until completion.

You may be assigned an Angel of love if you are going through relationship difficulties, or are about to be united with your life's soulmate, and healing Angels are sent for those who are poorly in some way.

Your designated Angels are sent to work exclusively with and beside you in particular circumstances and will always stay for as long as they are needed, so are, therefore, members of your Angel team as and when their "skills" and help are necessary or vital to you.

The Chorus

These helpful little Angels will 'chat away' to you and send you signs in many different ways to give you ideas and inspiration for all kinds of things.

They are often extremely creative and are very knowledgeable about a multitude of different subjects.

They will give you practical ideas too, which may lead you down a path which you would never ever have expected!

So now we have our team –
The Guardian Angel, the steadfast team members, the "pop-in" Angels and the chorus.

As you can see, you are constantly surrounded with help and support by many celestial beings – you are NEVER alone.

Trust that your Angels are there, and never be afraid to call on your team as they dearly love to be of assistance whenever they can – they will never be too busy to help you. If you're not too sure which member to call on, remember that they are working together to help you and you can be sure that just by requesting angelic assistance they will swiftly come to your aid.

Always remember that you have a role in this team also – Although the Angels will sometimes help us through celestial intervention they mostly help by sending us guidance. This can be through the many signs talked about in Chapter 3 or simply through angelically inspired intuition – that inner "knowing" that we all experience when faced with life's decisions, problems and choices.

Please remember to follow that guidance wherever you can as it will always be sent to help you in the best way possible!

Chapter 2

My Angel Team

My Guardian Angel

Although I have always been aware of my Guardian Angel's presence, feeling safe knowing he is near, I never really gave any thought to what his name may be until a couple of years ago. Nor did I have any concept of what he may look like until earlier this year when I was made aware of him in the most amazing experience!

First – his "official" name is Uriah. I was given his name whilst sitting quietly one evening in my Angel room. It was around twilight time and I was feeling very relaxed and content. I hadn't switched any lights on and the room was silent. I felt that my Guardian Angel was close and decided that it would be really lovely if I had a name that I could use whilst chatting with him – so I simply said "Guardian Angel, I know you're here, can you please tell me your name?".

Immediately, I was given the name "Uriah". It was very definite and was repeated to me several times for confirmation.

It's not a name that I have any known connection to, nor is it a name of any "fame" in the angelic world, but I accepted it as fact straight away. I had no reason at all to doubt it!

I still gave no real thought as to what Uriah looked like, but was just happy to accept his presence as always – that sense of security knowing he was there was enough for me.

However, in the early part of 2011 I was shown my Guardian Angel through an experience I can only describe as incredible – and totally unexpected.

I am a Reiki 2 practitioner and was feeling unwell myself, just generally tired and a bit run down, so decided to ask my Reiki Master, Jason for a full Reiki healing session.

The session was arranged for an evening in early spring. After a quick catch up chat with Jason I sat quietly in the chair with my eyes closed whilst Jason and I both connected to Reiki together. I was aware that Jason was standing in front of me with his arms stretched out towards me. Whilst he was doing this I felt a hand touch the back of my head. It was very gentle, and felt like a large hand resting on my hair. I felt that 'someone' was towering over me from behind. It felt wonderful and secure and lasted for about two minutes.

Soon after that moment it was time to climb up onto the couch for the healing session to begin and I settled down happily for what I knew was going to be something very special and powerful.

I often see "colours" when giving or having reiki and it was soon apparent that this session was completely pink! Although my eyes were closed I could see and sense that I was surrounded by a glowing pink light.

During the session I felt the large reassuring hand again twice – once on the top of my head and then the hand lingered for some time on my right arm. Both times I knew that Jason was not giving reiki to those parts of me – in fact he was near my legs and then my feet!

7

I knew that I had been touched by an Angel and that my Angel had a beautiful pink aura – a loving, rosy and protective glow.

Jason and I always discuss our experiences after reiki sessions and he told me before I left that he had seen a glowing infinity sign over my solar plexus area. He had felt an incredible energy in the room too. I was being shown how much I was loved (and always would be) at a time when I was feeling a bit low, and the whole experience lifted me in a way that I just cannot describe.

Going home that evening I felt truly blessed, not realising that more confirmation was to come that night.

After spending the evening in a state of angelically inspired euphoria, I took myself off to bed at about midnight. My partner, Bob, was working until 2am so I was alone.

As I was drifting off to sleep I had a wonderful vision of my Angel! My eyes were half closed and I saw him so clearly that I can still see that vision if I close my eyes today.

I knew instinctively that it was Uriah as all the pieces immediately 'came together' of everything that had happened during that unforgettable evening.

He is a really tall Angel and towers above me. He has blonde wavy short-ish hair – a bit like a Greek God image, and he has a woven crown on his head.

He's dressed in something very similar to a monk's robe but it is, of course, pink! Around his waist there is a cord, which hangs almost down to the floor.

He's beautiful and calming and fills me with a sense of safety and the security of being unconditionally loved.

He is my Guardian Angel.

Although the name I have been given for him is Uriah, I have affectionately named him "my big pink fella" and always now refer to him and address him that way!

I feel honoured that he chose to make himself known to me visually and let me experience his touch also. It is such a wonderful feeling to be able to visualise his presence by my side whenever and wherever we are, and I thank him often for being such a wonderful presence in my life.

My steadfast team members
Nana

I am the youngest of four children and soon after I was born my Mum became a single parent and we all went to live with my Nana who had been sadly widowed 2 years earlier, when in her early 50s.

For various reasons I spent a lot more of my time as a young child with my Nana than I did with my Mum and we formed a close bond.

My Mum re-married when I was 5 and we moved to a new home. As I grew up, my new step-sister and I were taken on holiday every year by my Nana to her sister Ethel's home just outside of London. Those holidays were the highlight of every summer for me. We must have seen every sight in London that there was to see! My Nana sadly died when I was 17 – my first experience of loss and I missed her dearly. I believe she handed over my earthly care to my future husband who I had met just a few months earlier.

Since I was first married, I have displayed an old black and white photograph of Nana, my sister and I in pride of place in my living room. We are standing in front of Hampton Court near London. I must have been about 8 yrs old in this picture – it's the only one I have of my Nana and I together and we are both holding little monkeys.

What stands out in the picture is that there is a glow around mine and Nana's hair – it gives me a sense of togetherness when I look at it – no other part of the picture has this particular glow.

Over the years I have talked to my Nana often, through good times and bad and have known that she would always help me if she could. Most things have always come right after calling on her, with the exception of when I asked her to help my husband recover at the time he was diagnosed with cancer in October 2002. Sadly he died only a month later and although I knew in my heart that there was nothing Nana could have done, I somehow felt deserted by the person I trusted to help as she always had.

I was devastated by the loss and seemed to lose my faith in her reassuring presence. I began to question my own beliefs and wondered if she was actually around me as I had always thought. I was asking myself if I had just imagined she was still with me for all those years. In the depths of grieving I couldn't feel her at all. I felt as though I had lost her along with my husband.

In early 2003 the trauma in my life continued, my step-dad and my beautiful first grandson died within the first 4 months of that year. Suffice to say, following 3 major losses I became very ill, suffered a break-down and was admitted voluntarily to hospital. Whilst there I unfortunately became worse instead of better, had very bad reactions to the combination of prescribed medications and being away from my home environment, and became increasingly reclusive, feeling totally hopeless, believing that I could never get any better or face up to life again.

I felt that nothing anyone was doing to try to "fix me" could possibly help. I just didn't know which way to turn.

On what I would describe as my worst night, my Nana appeared beside me in my room, and floated in and out of my vision for several minutes. She appeared younger than I had physically known her – more the age that I was myself, at that time - an image that I had seen in old photographs of her. Her face was surrounded in a white light and I was immediately comforted in her presence, aware from an "inner voice" that she was encouraging me to take control of my life again. My Nana had herself lost her husband and daughter (my aunt) at a relatively young age, and I knew that she was passing on her own strengths to me. I went to sleep knowing that I could get through the worst times and come out on the other side; I felt that I had been told what I should do and resolved to follow that guidance.

The next morning I took charge of my own destiny and asked to be taken off the majority of the medication and undertake grief counselling instead. It may not be the right course for everyone to take, but I just knew in my heart then that this was the right route for me.

I was discharged from the hospital within a week and with the wonderful counselling I was given, renewed faith in the future and pure determination over the next few months gradually became well again. I bought my first set of Angel Cards at that time – they helped me enormously.

I believe to this day that my Nana's love for me got me through a very dark period in my life, re-affirming my belief that I wasn't alone at a very crucial moment. I can't thank her enough for what she did for me that night and am so glad she is in my life.

Following my Guardian Angel, I feel that after so many years by my side that she is at the head of my team – my second Guardian, my friend and confidante.

John

John was my husband – father to my two children. We met on my 17th birthday, married two years later and lived a contented family life until he sadly passed away from cancer in 2002.

He was my soulmate – my best friend and I was secure and happy in the knowledge that we were a team. There was nothing that I wouldn't have trusted him with. He was a calm, laid back kind of man and always reassuring when things in life went wrong.

We only had a month to adjust to the fact that he was terminally ill as he had been mis-diagnosed by the family doctor as having "mild angina" following several visits in the year prior to his death. Losing John was like losing a part of myself.

I know when John is around me now as I feel a particular tingling sensation across my back, sometimes accompanied by the scent of "Brut" – a favourite after shave of his (and mine!) when we were younger. I first felt this sensation when returning home from the hospital the morning we lost him – it's as if he wanted me to know straight away that he was still with me. Although I wasn't sure at first what the sensation meant, I am absolutely sure now!

The family nick-name for John was "Mr Fixit" and he was excellent at mending or figuring out most things, particularly computers. I've asked him several times over the years for help when having problems with the pc or other technical things that I have thought beyond my comprehension – and he has always helped me through!

I also dream of John often – just in a natural way, nothing earth shattering – just that he is with me, chatting, so I know that he visits whilst I am asleep. This often happens when I am worried about something and I invariably see my way to a solution to problems soon after having these dreams. Sometimes I wake the next morning knowing exactly what I should do!

I know that the communication through dreams has been one of his many ways of helping and guiding me through all kinds of concerns over the years since we lost him.

I can still hear him today saying "Don't worry, hunnie, it will be alright!" and I know he is most definitely one my team of Angels!

Luke – the playful one!

Luke was my first grandson, who was born very poorly in April 2000 but managed to stay with us until April 2003.

Luke was unable to sit or walk so I am happy to say now that I have been told by a trusted medium that he was seen standing holding his grandad's hand whilst holding tigger – a favourite toy that his Mum & Dad chose to bury with him – in the other.

I have also had someone tell me that they have seen Luke running playfully around my legs.

How good it is to know that he's mobile and with his grandad too!

I believe that Luke calls in and has fun here hiding things from us, taking pleasure in watching us hunt for things – just because he can!

More steadfast members.....

My Mum – who confided in me a few months before she died that she had a vision of Jesus sitting with her on the side of a well at a Healing sanctuary she had visited. She spent time with me in a dream only recently, and both I and my daughter have detected her scent at the same moment – confirming her presence on numerous occasions.

Uncle Harold – who became a strong, protective and caring father figure to me when I needed one the most. Because of our mutual love of gardening, I believe he is my garden Angel - I would love to hear what he has to say about my fairy garden!

George – my paternal father who I never knew but has communicated to me through a

14

medium that he loves, cares and is around for me.

All of these people and more will never be gone in my eyes and I am so thankful they are part of my team and give me their input and guidance when the need arises.

My "Pop-in" Angels

Serena

Serena introduced herself to me through a spiritual healer friend. She initially came to me when I was writing my first set of Angel Cards and was sent specifically to help me with my work involving the angelic realm – to help me bring angelic guidance and more to many other people, in the form of the written word.

Although I personally hadn't seen Serena (my friend did!) I already knew that I was receiving guidance and celestial channelling whilst creating the cards as everything came together with them so easily. The words for each card flowed effortlessly every time I sat down to write!

Although being told that Serena was with me didn't come as a huge surprise, it was wonderful confirmation of angelic support in my new venture – and so nice to have her name, too.

I have since written a second set of cards (which will hopefully be published this year) – again with Serena's help and I'm sure that she's standing right beside me now as I am writing this book!

My Chorus

I call these my chatterbox Angels! I don't have individual names for them but see them as a group of three young-ish 'wispy' females, always together, almost in a huddle as if they are confiding in each other and me, too.

They are a very lively trio, always chatting and smiling – the "creativity" team.

Many of the creative ideas I have had for the home have come from these lovely girls, I am sure.

They love to impart new imaginative thoughts and insights, also giving me inspiration for new material to be added to the websites all the time. Every time I think that I have completed the sites, my head will suddenly be filled with new ideas.

It's so lovely to know that these happy little Angels have helped me to build the websites which are helping so many people from all over the world with their spiritual journeys.

Their inspiration is definitely heaven sent!

Now you know who is on my team, try putting pen to paper and making a list of who may be on yours – you will be surprised at how easy it will be for you to figure out – with a little help from your Angel friends!

Chapter 3

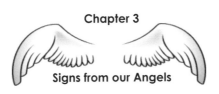

Signs from our Angels

How wonderful it is when we receive signs from our Angels! Whether it signifies a visitation from a lost loved one or simply confirms the delight of having angelic presence in our lives, these signs can boost our spirits enormously.

Sometimes we will be sent a sign when we've asked for one, but more often we'll see them at the most unexpected moments. These moments frequently coincide with our times of need – and our Angels send us a sign of hope to get us through a difficult period.

Occasionally they'll send us a sign just because they can and they know how happy it makes us to receive their 'calling cards'.

These celestial signs can come in hundreds of different forms as they can be something very personal to the recipient.

Here I've listed those that I think are the Angels' most familiar ways of alerting us to their presence. Some have my own personal experiences within them, others have inspiring anecdotes that I have been sent by other people.

How many of the following signs do you think you may have experienced?

Angel Shapes

Shapes of Angels can appear almost anywhere! From the bubbles in your bath to the flowers in your garden.

You may see the form of a complete Angel, or maybe just a pair of Angel wings. You don't have to go looking for them as you can be sure that if your Angels are trying to alert you to their presence you will be looking in just the right place at exactly the right time.

"I have a rose quartz crystal heart that I've owned for about ten years. Last week I decided to hold the heart up to the light for some reason, and then saw the shape of an Angel inside it which I had never seen before! The heart is even more special to me now." ~ Simone

Butterflies

Wow – what a beautiful sign a butterfly is! It is often seen as a sign of emerging or a new beginning – just as the butterfly emerges from the chrysalis.

Being visited by a butterfly is also synonymous with being visited by a lost loved one.

Recently I visited Tintagel in Cornwall and decided to take the huge walk up the cliff steps to the very top of the site of Tintagel castle. It was a beautiful, hot and sunny day and after spending some time down on the beach enjoying the waterfall and visiting Merlin's cave (magical!), we started the daunting climb up to the cliff summit.

Now, I'm not 20 any more and have achy knees at the best of times, so was dubious about the climb (said to be over 300ft), especially when looking upwards from the shore! However, I can also be quite determined and was sure that I could achieve it with a few little "rest stops" on the way.

Right from the start of the climb I was accompanied by a red admiral butterfly. It was flying by my right side all along the way and when I stopped for a "breather" it hovered near me every time until I set off again. I was aware of it for the entire climb.

On getting to the top I decided to go into the old castle "lady's garden" and the butterfly hovered with me there. As I sat down on the grass I noticed a perfectly formed small white feather which I picked up and kept. When I looked back up my butterfly friend had gone.

I believe that my butterfly companion was sent by my late husband, John, who absolutely adored Cornwall too, to see me safely and happily to the uppermost point where my white feather was waiting for me – showing me clearly that I had been accompanied by one of my Angels that day.

"I was struggling and stressing about life whilst on one of my keep fit runs, when a butterfly appeared at my shoulder and flew with me for a good five minutes" ~ Theresa

"I was feeling a bit low and asked the Angels to give me a sign that they were around me. The very next day I saw 10 white butterflies flying together alongside my hedge." ~ Kyla

"I asked for a sign that my lovely Dad, who had passed ten years earlier, was still close by. I asked to be shown something that I wouldn't expect to see. It was the middle of January and a freezing cold day with a bitter wind. A short while after asking for a sign I walked into the

kitchen and saw a black butterfly fluttering outside the window. It stayed for a few seconds before flying straight up into the air and disappearing" ~ Carol

Car number plates (license plates)
I have always made up names for cars we have owned – using the letters on the plate as the basis for the name – just a bit of fun really. When buying a new car recently, we went to see one that had the letters GLY on the front of the plate. My immediate thought was "ugly"! It turned out the salesman was definitely not reputable and on examining the car we found that it had a lot of hidden problems. Suffice to say we didn't buy it!

On a more serious note though, number plates can be used as a way of relaying messages to us and you will probably have found yourself following a car at some point with letters or numbers on the plate which have made you think of someone or something that you should be doing, or even given you reassurance in a time of need as they did with Angela in the quote below:

"I got a call telling me that my father passed away and left Nevada to drive to California. As I was driving over the mountain I thought that I really should not be driving. The license plate on the car in front of me said ART. Art was the name of my grandfather who I was very close to that had already passed. I knew at that moment I would be ok and that my grandfather was with my dad. That car stayed with me till the end of my trip." ~ Angela

Clouds

When you are sitting quietly in the garden, the park or on the beach and get an urge to look heavenwards, take the time to see what you can spot amongst the clouds.

I have seen Angel wings, feathers and even entire Angels looking down on me from above in the form of clouds!

I have also heard of people seeing hearts, initials and many other things too.

Take a look – your Angels are very creative and will use many ways like this to get your attention, sending you signs of love and reassurance from their heavenly domain.

"I see Angel shapes in the clouds all the time. One night 2 years ago I saw a staircase in the clouds. It looked just like the stairway to heaven." ~ Moira

"I need only to look at your Angel Cards, MJ, the face says it all" ~ Sharyn (referring to the face that appears amongst the clouds in my "Pocketful of Angels" deck when the cards are turned upside down – as this was not intentional!)

"I see x's in the sky often and know that they are kisses from my Angels" ~ Claire

Coins

"Pennies from heaven".

You've probably heard the phrase 'See a penny pick it up and all day long you'll have good luck'. So when you come across a coin unexpectedly in your path, do just that!

Our Angels drop 'pennies' in our path to remind us they are there, also to send you luck in some form just when you may need it.

It is always worth checking the date on any coins you find too, as it may bear some importance to someone you have loved and lost and the coin could be a special sign for you from them.

If you see someone drop a coin – pick it up and give it back to them, remembering that any kindness will come back to you two-fold.

"I was worried as my daughter was going on a boat trip to France and I'd had a very sleepless night because of it. The next morning I went out into the garden and guess what I found together on the patio? A French franc with a white feather! From that moment on I knew that I had absolutely nothing to worry about." ~ Lisa

Dreams

It is my firm belief that our Angels and lost loved ones visit us whilst we sleep. This is because they know that this is when we are at our most relaxed and receptive. Also there are no outside influences to distract us.

In my experience the dreams are quite ordinary! It may be that you will dream of taking a companionable walk, a drive in the car or having a nice chat about all manner of every day subjects.

Whatever form the dream takes, it's their presence that's important. The fact that they are still with you shines through, so don't try to analyse or interpret what the dream could mean – just be happy that you've enjoyed the company and spent some time with someone that you miss being with. If they have come with the purpose of giving you a message or imparting some guidance you will remember what that was upon waking for sure.

If, in the morning, you find that they have left you a "calling card" of some kind as confirmation by the side of your bed then that will give you an extra feeling of peace too, safe in the knowledge that it really wasn't "just a dream".

"I dreamt that my deceased husband was with me and when I woke up in the morning I found a pure white feather on my dressing gown next to the bed – his way of letting me know the dream was real." ~ Mary

Images within images

Have you ever taken a photograph and then seen an Angel or other kindly face within the image once it has been developed or downloaded?

Only recently I took a photo of the healing waterfall at Chalice Well gardens in Glastonbury and was happy to find no less than three definite Angel outlines within the image! Given the incredible feeling of peace in the wonderful atmosphere at the healing gardens, I was not surprised at all that I had been blessed with the company of Angels whilst there.

It shows that we are surrounded by far more than our eyes can always see. Angels and other beings presenting themselves to us through our photographs is an excellent way for them to let us know they are here when we may not otherwise have seen them.

Further confirmation for me of how celestial beings will unexpectedly appear in an image is on my own set of Angel message cards "A Pocketful of Angels" which were published in 2010. I had worked closely with the graphic designer, Matt, whilst creating the design of the beautiful Angel soaring through heavenly skies. Understandably, our main concern was to get the Angel "just right" – the surrounding skies being purely a complimentary background.

Shortly after publishing the cards I received an excited e-mail from a facebook friend, Sharyn, in Australia who had been one of the first people to purchase them. She asked me about the image that she could see in the clouds when she had turned the cards upside down!

I had no idea what she was referring to until I tried it – and there, as clear as anything is a face in the clouds! I contacted Matt who was as surprised as I was. He said that he had drawn the clouds free-hand beneath the Angel, believing them to be "just" clouds and he had no idea that the face was there either. He tells me now that the experience of making this discovery has completely changed his perception of the angelic realms and that he is now a firm believer!

"I took a picture of my daughter sitting at the kitchen table. In the picture there is an Angel behind my daughter, I can clearly see the wings and body shape on the wall" ~ Lupe

24

Lights

Have you ever seen twinkling or sparkling lights out of the corner of your eye? It is almost a sensation of "did I really see that?" and is an indication that an Angel is beside you.

Depending on the colour these could be sent by an Archangel whose help you are in need of at that time. For instance, green sparkles may indicate the presence of Archangel Raphael at a time when you are in need of healing, blue sparkles could be a sign that Archangel Michael is bringing you some extra strength or protection and twinkling pink lights may be due to a loving embrace being directed towards you from Archangel Chamuel.

Some people have reported seeing rainbow colours or pure white light surrounding their Angels, others have seen an entire room light up with a warm glow.

Isn't it lovely how Angels can literally light up our lives?

"I was going through a stressful period in my life recently and while taking a shower I asked my Angels to please help me. Nothing happened immediately but when stepping into the hall after taking my shower I noticed that there was a very peaceful orange glow going all the way through the house. It was everywhere I looked, and only I could see it! I knew it was the Angels and felt incredibly reassured." ~ Pia

Magazines and Books

Sometimes when the answer to a problem is evading us, the Angels will send us messages through the written word in the best way they can.

It could be that you'll see a book or magazine with a particular title or cover story that will give you an answer, this may stand out on a shelf or even fall at your feet as you are passing.

Also you can ask for a solution to be sent by communicating your question to the Angels. You can do this either out loud or in your head, then open your chosen book or magazine at random, trusting that your angelically guided instinct is taking you to the right page. Now look at the page – is there a sentence, word, phrase or article that jumps out at you?

You never know, it may be just the help you need!

"Following a difficult relationship break up I was feeling very low and terribly alone. When out shopping one day there was a sudden thunderstorm and I took shelter in the local charity shop. When I was in there I was drawn to a book which was on the shop counter. The book was all about Angels, I hadn't really given them much thought before. I bought the book and after reading just the first chapter I realised that our Angels are always around us and I haven't felt lonely since. I am so glad that it thundered that day!" ~ *Stephen*

Music and Television
Hearing a song or lyric on the radio featuring words that help, reassure or confirm something for you is never a coincidence, but rather the work of your Angels helping you find solutions to troubling situations, or even guidance towards

something new or different that they'd like you to embrace in your life.

If you hear a song repeatedly then please try and figure out why this may be happening as it will have been sent to help you in some way.

It may not always be the words of a song that are significant; it could be the name of the artist that holds importance.

Could it be the name of someone you have lost who is letting you know they are there for you?

Is it possible that the group who are singing the song are or were a favourite of somebody special in your life?

Similarly with television, you could be flicking channels and come across something by chance that helps you at that time. A documentary or show with a particular theme or name that you feel you need to stop and watch for a moment might hold an important message for you. Always be open to the possibilities of your Angels communicating through the media this way – you could be very happily surprised!

"I had been crying whilst sitting in the garden, worrying that I couldn't get through a difficult situation. As I walked back indoors I heard 'I will survive' on the radio – that gave me hope" ~ Anon

Rainbows

… are quite rare and we all delight in seeing them. When you see one you should think of it as the Angels sending down a little bit of heaven. They love to share their beautiful realm with us however they can. A rainbow when there has been no rain holds particular significance with its unexpected radiance as it defies logical reason as to why it would be there for us to see.

"Whilst relaxing on the beach on a beautiful sunny day and writing about Angels, I looked up and saw that the sun was totally encircled by a rainbow – a stunning sight! A sign that the Angels liked what I was writing." ~ Mary Jac

Repetitive words and phrases

Do you ever find yourself hearing the same person's name, a place name, number or phrase several times in a day from many different sources?

It may be that you hear it by chance from people chatting as they pass you in the street.

You might then hear that same thing again whilst in a shop, then on the radio or tv – the possibilities are endless!

If you do notice this kind of repetitiveness you should pay attention to the messages that your Angels are trying to send you and the guidance that will be within these messages. You can be sure that they will have been sent to help you in some significant way.

Trust that your first instinct when thinking of what the Angels are trying to communicate will be the right one and take heed of their advice when you can!

"I had been thinking about doing a college course but kept putting it off. Everywhere I went it seemed that I heard references to studying, books, learning new skills etc. I said "okay, okay!" and finally enrolled on the course. I'm overjoyed to say that I met my future husband there – he was the tutor! " ~ Jenny

Road names, buildings, advertising slogans

Have you ever been thinking about something or someone, and then seen their name on some kind of sign as you have driven down the road? Or maybe you have called on Archangel Michael for help and then noticed a church called "St Michaels" shortly after – his way of letting you know he has heard you.

Pay attention to any recurring names or slogans that catch your eye on advertising billboards, neon signs, road names and shop names too. If you are being prompted in some way to see them there will be a message there for you somewhere!

"Mary, we were in Ibiza because we had to do some healing and I asked Archangel Michael to help me. I was thinking of your feature as I did it and the fact that Angels will often send us signs to let us know they have heard us. Right after doing it, we were driving somewhere and instantly drove past a place called St Miguel and then the next day my card for the day was Michael! If I'd had your email address, I would have emailed you right there and then!" ~ *Golnaz Alibagi – deputy editor, 'Soul & Spirit' magazine* (referring to my Angel Signs article in the magazine July 2011)

"I was thinking of my deceased sister-in-law, Rafaelina and how much I missed her. As I was walking along a white feather fell in front of me, then when I looked up from seeing that I immediately saw a van with RAFAEL sign-written on it. I'm sure she was letting me know that she was with me that day." ~ *Rosie*

29

Robins

A robin is said to bring the spirits of lost loved ones to visit you. You will often find the same robin will visit your garden year after year.

We had one visit our garden three years running after losing my Mum until we moved home – I truly believe it was her!

More recently my partner, Bob, caught sight of a robin when we were visiting Chalice Well Gardens in Glastonbury. He tried to point the robin out to me but when I turned around it had gone, so this robin was there to see Bob, I am sure.

His immediate thought was that his Dad was saying 'hello' and I'm positive he was right!

"The day after my husband died my daughter and I drove from Fife down to Lockerbie where my husband had been renting a cottage whilst working there. When we arrived to collect his belongings, the most beautiful rainbow I have ever seen appeared. When I opened the door to the cottage a robin redbreast flew in and settled on my husband's work fleece which was on the couch. What a great comfort it was to have signs that he was with us that day." ~ Fiona

Scents and smells

An Angel will often be accompanied by a sweet floral scent, often lavender, but it could be of any flower at all. I've been told by friends that they have detected the scent of gardenias, roses, freesias, honeysuckle, and numerous other flowers too.

The scent will not necessarily be associated with anyone you once knew, but will be strong enough to make you stop what you are doing and take notice – yet another way that the Angels will use to alert you to their presence.

Sometimes those we have lost will waft their own fragrance towards you too. It could be anything from their own distinctive perfume to the smell of baking cakes if they had well been known for their cooking skills.

Even my husband, who was a little bit unsure about these things, used to say that he knew when my Mum was around after she had passed away as he could "smell" her scent too.

"I lived somewhere with a heavy energy and I was very sad and distressed. One night I walked into my room and as I did I could smell this amazing smell, like cookies baking but 300 times better! I then felt sudden warmth and a feeling of overwhelming love. The experience lifted me and gave me peace where there had been none before. ~ Lisa

Telephone calls/visits

Have you ever been feeling a bit low, lonely or unwell and then received a totally unexpected phone call or visit from a friend or family member?

Sometimes our Angels will, when they see us in need, send us someone to help to cheer us by giving them a little "nudge" by planting a seed in their minds to encourage them to get in touch.

Sometimes people will contact you in some way simply for a chat – at a time when you could just do with some company, other times they will get in touch to offer their friendly support at a significant moment.

They may bring some angelically prompted wisdom or clarity for you too, passing on celestial advice or guidance to help you through a difficult time.

This is why people often seem to contact us at just the right moment – it isn't coincidence - they have been sent by our Angels!

"I was feeling very low after the death of my husband and asked the Angels to send me something, anything to make me feel a bit better. At that point an old friend of my mother called me, I hadn't heard from her for a long time and it was so good to hear her voice. She told me that when pulling out the hall table she had found an old letter from my mum sticking out of the back of the drawer and it had made her think of me. She felt that she was being told to contact me by my mum, who had died several years previously. I think she was right. " ~ Anon

Touch

An Angels' touch is usually fleeting and gentle, although it can sometimes last for a few minutes.

You may feel a hand resting lightly on your head or touching your arm, or experience a tingling sensation across your back as I have.

Some people have reported the wonderful sensation of feeling touched by and wrapped in an Angel's wings.

To feel the touch of an Angel is one of the most beautiful things you can experience and I think that those of us who have been lucky enough to do so have been well and truly blessed.

"I have felt the Angels playing with my hair" ~ Sarah

A Voice
Your Angels may have spoken to you out loud, or just in a little whisper. You may hear your name called when there is nobody else in the house, or you may hear a short reassuring message. You could also be given a little bit of guidance this way.

Perhaps you may even get an instruction telling you to do something immediately as Kimberly did below.

"One day after learning that I could ask for signs, and being in a very difficult place I asked the Angels to send me a sign that I couldn't miss or misunderstand. I was reading in the car waiting for my son to finish soccer and heard a voice saying "look up". In the sky was the hugest cloud that looked exactly like a gigantic white feather!" ~ Kimberly W

"After my hubby Jim died I felt that I just didn't want to carry on. I was lying in bed one night in a terrible emotional state when I felt someone take my hand. I then heard a voice saying 'Linda, it's me, Jim. You must look forward now and everything will be okay'. Although it was strange it was such a good feeling and I know it was real" ~ Linda

White feathers

I have been blessed with white feathers so many times now that I could probably write a whole book just about them!

When I first started to write this book whilst on holiday in Cornwall I went up to the roof terrace for a break on what was a very windy evening and as I opened the skylight door to climb out a perfect white feather was dancing down right in front of me – side to side, very slowly and seemingly not caught up in the wind at all. It was almost as though it was making sure it got my attention. I saw it as celestial approval that I was finally putting pen to paper and getting this book underway!

In the past I have stepped out of my front door to see white feathers on the doorstep, looked up from reading to see one floating past the living room window and even found them stuck to my clothes! Even at the tender age of three, my grandson, Charlie, is becoming aware. On finding one together the other day he asked if he could please put it in his pocket and keep it because "the Angels love us, Nana" and proudly showed his mummy what we'd found when we arrived home!

White feathers will not always appear when you ask for them, but often manifest at meaningful moments or in a place when you would least expect to find one.

One of the best known "calling cards" of the Angels, they are a sent as a sign that we are loved, protected and never alone. They can be sent to assure us that we are on the right path, making the correct decision or simply as a show of angelic support at a significant time.

Our lost loved ones will send them to say "hey, I'm still with you!", too – how wonderful is that?

"Last year whilst gardening, I was thinking of my mother who has passed as she also enjoyed gardening. When I turned around there was a white feather in one of my potplants!" ~ Brenda

"My Aunty died suddenly last year. It was the day of the funeral and I went to get dressed, ready to go. I found a beautiful white feather tucked amongst the clothes I was sorting out to wear. It was very comforting for me on a difficult day." ~ Josie

At the beginning of this chapter I mentioned Angelic signs that are often unique or personal to the individual receiving them.
Here's a few of the more personal signs that I have been told about:

"When I was very sick in hospital I woke up to see the image of an awesome white Angel appear on the wall" ~ Christina

"About 5 years ago we were trying without success to sell our house and I was becoming desperate. I had recently become interested in spirituality - reiki and crystals etc and at around 4am one morning I woke up to the most beautiful angelic choir music that I have ever heard. I felt so at peace. A couple of months later the house was sold" ~ Lin

"Sadly, we had to have our dog, Sam put to sleep and I asked the Angels for a sign that

would show me he was okay and had passed over peacefully. Two days later our house plant bloomed one single lily. My parents had owned this plant for 25 years and it had never flowered before! I believed that this was the sign I had asked for from the Angels to let me know that Sam was at peace and found it very comforting." ~ Nina

"I had asked a question, and then asked for a sign. I wasn't particular about what kind of sign, but when it happened, I knew. I had a hanging plant out on the porch, it did have petunias in it for the summer, but by that November, it was just the brown empty stems hanging over the side of the pot. The next morning, I went out on the porch, and it was totally green, full of just bloomed petunias." ~ Helena

"It was my first pregnancy, and I was having a hard time. I had lost one twin and prayed and prayed not to lose the other. My Grandmother, who had passed when I was 17, came to me in a dream. She told me to stop fussing, calm down that my baby would be fine. That baby girl is now twenty-one and a lovely young lady!" ~ Shelia

Chapter 4

How our Angels can help us
The A-Z of Angelic Assistance

There are so many ways that your Angels can and will help you. Remember that they take great delight in assisting us – all you have to do is ask!

This chapter will give you some insight into the more 'common place' things that you may be seeking guidance with and indicates, too, which of the Archangels you can call on for assistance. Each section here also has a positive affirmation you can use if you wish to as well. Positivity is something our Angels take great delight in and they'd love to know that you feel that way too.

You will find a few things here that you may not have thought you could ask for celestial help with, but your ever helpful Angel team may surprise you all the same.

Abundance

Most of us have known the worry of not being able to make ends meet at some point and I have found that when I have asked my team for help with this, then something invariably comes to me in some form!

No – I haven't won the lottery! But have often had either small unexpected cheques arrive in the post or have had an angelically inspired idea which has given me the means to see me through.

If you feel that you would like to call on an Archangel for guidance with financial issues, call upon Archangel Ariel – the Angel of abundance.

Affirmation: "I believe that all my needs will be met"

Belief
We all get our 'down' days at times and I get a lot of mail from people who are fearful that their Angels have deserted them.
When we are feeling low it can sometimes be difficult to 'hear' what our Angels are trying to communicate because our minds can be over-run with negative thoughts.
We can also easily miss the signs they are sending us if we are focusing on everything that is wrong in our lives.
If you find yourself feeling like this try to focus only on the positive aspects of your life and believe that things WILL get better for you.
Ask Archangel Michael to help you to restore your faith and call on your Angel team to find ways to show you the way forward. Ask them to show you how you can improve your situation, then be open to the help and guidance they'll be sure to send you – because they will!

Affirmation: "I believe that everything can and will get better"

Creativity
If you're looking for help with an artistic project, such as painting or creative writing, ask for the assistance of Archangel Gabriel who will help

you awaken and channel your creative potential.

If it is a musical talent that you are looking to expand on then you should send your prayers to Archangel Sandalphon who loves to hear us singing and playing musical instruments. (Sandalphon is also the Archangel known for carrying our prayers to God.)

Remember to call upon your own Angel team as well, asking them to help you find the correct outlet for your given talent. They will be sure to find ways to give you pointers towards any study courses or learning tools you may need, too.

Affirmation: "I have confidence in my ability to express myself through my creativity"

Decisions

Making decisions can sometimes be very hard and we can find ourselves totally stuck between two choices.

When you find yourself in this kind of dilemma, call upon your Angels to help quieten your mind and then try to visualise exactly how you would feel if you were now living with the result of each different choice in turn.

The Angels will work with you through your intuition and will assist you with your "gut" instincts, telling you intuitively which path you should take – give it a try!

Affirmation: "I am the master of my destiny with the Angels as my allies"

Enthusiasm

Archangel Haniel is the one to call on when you are lacking in energy or enthusiasm to ask that your zest for life be restored.

You can also ask members of your team to find inventive ways to steer you towards something new and interesting by means of a sign, such as those talked about in Chapter 3. They are sure to think of something that will renew your passion for life – then prepare to be amazed by the new ideas they will communicate to you.

Affirmation: "I believe that my life is a wonderful adventure with many exciting experiences yet to come"

Finding lost items

How often have you lost an item in the home and, despite searching 'everywhere', still cannot find it?

Next time that happens try this:

Calm down and stand still for a moment, then say "Angels, please can I have my (lost item) back?"

Then go to wherever your instinct directs you to, even if you're sure that you have looked there already and I would be willing to bet that 99 times out of every 100 you'll find your item.

It definitely works for me.

The chances are that someone on your Angel team was being playful with you by hiding the item in the first place. As soon as you ask politely for it back they'll direct you right to it.

Oh – and don't forget to thank them when you find it, they love good manners just as much as we do.

Affirmation: "I'm blessed by and embrace the connection that I have with my Angels"

Grieving
… is a very hard process and can take a long time to get through with many set backs along the way.

Archangel Azrael not only helps our lost ones through the transition to the heavenly realms but will comfort you through your period of mourning too.

He will appoint an Angel to stay with you for as long as you need them if you just ask for his help, so please don't ever think that you have to go through these awful times alone.

Affirmation: "I will take small but sure steps towards the future"

Healing
The Archangel whose purpose it is to help us heal both physically and emotionally is Archangel Raphael. Call on him whenever you need to and ask for his comfort and healing.

Although we all know that healing miracles both large and small can definitely occur (you only have to read some of the stories towards the end of this book to confirm that), it is more likely that he will guide you through ways to help you heal yourself. You may, for instance, get a strong urge to cut out/release something or someone from your life to assist the healing process.

Or he may lead you to think of alternative therapies which will greatly benefit you, or send an Earth Angel your way who will help you to heal.

You can be sure that whatever he sends, it will be only be for your highest good and optimal health.

Never think that this or any other Archangel will be too busy to hear your prayers, he will always be there for you.

Affirmation: "I believe that a worrisome situation can be healed"

Ideas and Inspiration

Are you looking for new ideas for your home or business and feeling decidedly uninspired?

If you've been driving yourself mad trying to think of something, or have just hit a 'mental block', try the following:

Find yourself a spare half an hour to take yourself off into a quiet room – somewhere that you can relax (the bath always works for me).

Lie down, close your eyes and empty your mind of all "every day" thoughts.

Try not to think of all those things that you feel you should be doing, just take some time out to allow the inspiration to flow.

Now, simply ask Archangel Uriel and the members of your Angel team to send you the inspiration you need and open your mind to allow ideas to form – it really is that simple!

You may get an immediate idea, or the Angels may send you the inspiration over the following weeks through one of the many signs listed earlier in this book.

Either way, you will find your imagination being stimulated in ways you may never previously have thought of.

Affirmation: "I trust that divine inspiration will come my way"

Job Interviews

Archangel Chamuel is the one who helps us with all career matters as well as being the Archangel to call on when we need an extra bit of confidence.

If you're going for a job interview, or being considered for promotion at work, then this kind and gentle Angel is definitely the one to call on.

As with any stressful or difficult appointment you can always ask a member of your Angel team to accompany you, then visualise them sitting by your side supporting you there at all moments of difficulty or uncertainty. You'll be amazed at how much more confidence this can give you.

Affirmation: "I have the ability within me to deal with stressful situations"

Keeping safe

Call upon Archangel Michael for this one. He is the leader of all Archangels and will protect you both physically and emotionally too.

Ask him to wrap you protectively in the safety of his royal blue cloak. Then visualise him there surrounding you in his aura, holding his sword by his side warding off anything or anyone who may harm you.

You can use this visualisation for any situation where you feel worried or threatened by anything, and be secure in the knowledge that he will be there shielding you with his loving care.

43

Affirmation: "I trust that I am safe and protected at all times"

Love

Whether it's self love, attracting the love of others or finding your soulmate you can ask for Archangel Chamuel's assistance with this.

He will also help you to find ways to mend relationships that may have been going through difficulties.

All Angels want us to be happy and none more so than the Angels on your own team, so you can be sure they will do everything they can to assist you with relationship happiness too.

Create a loving atmosphere in your home by surrounding yourself with anything that represents love to you, whether it's flowers, music, dimmed lighting or anything else that makes you feel enveloped by love in your own surroundings.

Then call upon Archangel Chamuel and your team to bring you the love in your life that you both want and deserve. Talk to them, tell them your needs and desires and ask that they direct you towards fulfilling and loving relationships.

* Tip: A large chunk of rose quartz in the house is excellent for attracting love into your home. Ask Archangel Chamuel to bless the stone for you and then ensure that you place it within view of the front door.

Affirmation: "I rejoice in the knowledge that I am lovable and loved"

Manifestation

We can manifest good things into our lives simply by being positive and believing that they will come to us.

This applies to all aspects of your lives, including emotional well-being and material possessions.

Think of the things that would make you truly happy in your life, imagine that your Angels are all around you (because they are!) and affirm to them your belief that good things can and will happen for you.

Your Angels will take great delight in your positivity and you will soon find that by thinking, affirming and believing you CAN be happier/achieve goals and more, they will help you do just that.

Affirmation: "I believe I can achieve anything that I want to"

Nurturing yourself

You should take time out daily (even if it's only ten minutes) to relax and connect with your Angels, asking them to help you to relax and re-charge.

Spending just a short time each day in gentle angelic meditation will do you the world of good, and who knows what guidance you may open to hearing when you allow yourself to relax in this way!

Affirmation: "I give myself the gift of relaxation and self care"

Organisation

If you are lacking in organisation and need a guiding hand with this, ask Archangel Metatron to help you to structure your time.

He will also give you the necessary motivation to get things running smoothly in your life.

Affirmation: "I take pleasure from ensuring I have order in my life"

Parking

Have you heard of the "Parking Angels"?

Next time you go shopping or on any other outing and want to avoid the stress of circling whilst looking for somewhere to park, ask the Angels to find you a space in the busy street or car park. You'll be amazed at how often they will oblige.

You can also apply the same principle to requesting they direct you to the shortest queue in a supermarket!

Affirmation: "I am blessed with angelic assistance in all ways"

Quarrels

If you find yourself frequently involved in family arguments or disputes, Archangel Raguel is the one who will help to smooth things over.

He loves to assist us with family unison and mutual co-operation and he will do all he can to make our home lives more harmonious.

Call on him whenever you need to for guidance, asking him to show you ways to strengthen family unity and bring peace into the home.

Affirmation: "I trust that harmony will prevail"

Releasing the past
… can make us so much more content and ready to embark on a brighter future. It isn't good for us to hold on to people or situations that make us unhappy and our Angel teams will work with us to let things go if we just ask them!
The lost loved ones on our teams don't want to see us unhappy any more than they would have done in life so will take great joy in steering us towards future happiness.
Look out for the guidance they are sure to be sending you to lead you to brighter times.
If you need extra help cutting the ties which are holding you back ask Archangel Michael to assist you by cutting through them with his sword.
Remember that each new day can be a fresh start if you allow yourself to move forward. Embrace all the new experiences and people you encounter with the thought that it will bring smiles to the faces of your Angel team when you do.

Affirmation: "I release the past knowing that my future will now be bright"

Sleeping
Many of us go through stages in life where we have trouble sleeping. Sometimes this is due to worrying about something, or our minds buzzing with ideas, but it can just be a cycle we can get in to which is difficult to break.
One tip I can pass on to you, as a person who is often wakeful myself, is to call on your Angel

team for some celestial company, then visualise yourself holding your Angel's hand – you can even reach out your hand and 'feel' it cradled in theirs.

If you want to call on an Archangel when you are having sleeping difficulties ask Archangel Azrael to come to you and gently lull you to sleep.

Affirmation: "I will sleep tonight with the gentle company of my Angels"

Travelling

We already know that Archangel Raphael is the Angel of healing, but did you know that he is also the Archangel of travelling?

Ask him before a journey to help make everything go smoothly for you, whether you are driving, flying or using any other public transport.

You could request that there are not too many traffic hold ups, that your flight runs on time, or even that you manage to get a seat on the train.

You can also ask Archangel Michael to keep you safe and protected on your journey. With two Archangels looking after you, you should arrive safely at your destination – and right on time, too!

Affirmation: "I trust that my journey will be safe and stress free"

Uncertainty

We often need help sorting out our feelings and sometimes just chatting to a friend will help us to see things more clearly.

However, there are times when we feel that we cannot openly voice our feelings to other people and that's when our Angels come in.

You will probably know which member of your Angel team you'd like to voice your worries to and it could help you enormously to do just that. Simply talk to them as you would have done in life, either out loud or by 'transmitting' your thoughts to them in a chatty kind of way.

It may be that the simple process of getting things off your chest in this way will be enough to clarify things for you – if not, you can always ask them to send you clear signs or guide you through the thinking process to give you the clarity that has been evading you.

If you feel the need for intervention or assistance from an Archangel, then Archangel Raguel is the one to appeal to for help.

Affirmation: "I believe that my way ahead will soon become clear"

Visualisation

It can help us through many situations to simply visualise our Angels beside us or accompanying us to difficult appointments or events that we may be worried about.

I have visualised my own Guardian Angel sitting in the back of the car on the way to the dentists! Whatever the situation, members of our Angel teams will always be with us. Remind yourself of that wherever you are and that thought will help you get through just about anything.

Affirmation: "I am surrounded by my Angel team at all times"

Weather

Now this is one that I have tried myself when I was on holiday. We arrived on a Friday and the first couple of days were beautiful – as per the forecast. Then all forecasts said that the weather would change from the Tuesday afternoon to heavy rain, cold winds and storms which would last right through to the end of the week.

I asked the Angels on the Monday night if they could please possibly improve on that so that we could continue to enjoy the beach and the relaxation of being outdoors, as our holiday in the same place last year had been a total wash out, with pouring rain every single day.

And guess what?

Although it rained heavily during that night, and with the exception of one wet afternoon on the Wednesday, the rest of the week was gorgeous, allowing us to enjoy the beach and the fresh air.

I know these kind of requests can't be granted all of the time, but it just shows that anything is worth a try – thank you Angels!

Affirmation: "I trust that my Angels always do their best for me"

Xmas and other **Y**early occasions

As with any family occasion or anniversary, the lost loved ones on your Angel team are sure to be with you.

Although these events can be very poignant and give rise to a few tears, it is also good for us to know that our loving Angels are around us and always will be.

Wish them a happy day and take pleasure in the fact that they will be delighted to see you and the rest of the family having fun and enjoying yourselves.

Affirmation: "I am secure in the knowledge that my lost loved ones are still with me"

Zadkiel
Is the Archangel who can help you with forgiveness and clarity.
He can also help you with psychological healing. Call on him when you need an extra someone to help soothe you through times of emotional trauma.
He'll do all he can to help you regain your contentment and peace of mind.
As with everyone on your Angel team, all he wants is to see you happy!

Affirmation: "My inner strength is amazing and will carry me through"

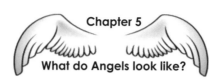

Chapter 5

What do Angels look like?

We will all see our Angels differently. 99% of the images you may come across in books, magazines etc will have all Angels depicted as beings with wings, but this isn't necessarily the case.

The lost loved ones members of our teams will usually appear to us just as they were, although they may now choose to appear looking as they did at an age when they were the happiest on earth. For instance, your grandmother who may have passed over when 86 years old and was crippled with arthritis at the time, may choose to appear as she was at 36 years old when she was content and pain free – or, if she thinks it may help you, she will come to you at an age when you perhaps remember her in the most reassuring way for you, so would be comforted by seeing her as she was then.

Some people see their Angels as beings of light, shadows, orbs and numerous other forms – the possibilities are endless! These quotes from Lu and Mel are both interesting and very perceptive:

"I believe that Angels will look like whatever you want them to look like. They appear however you feel most comfortable seeing them; whatever won't make you feel scared or insecure. If the human form is what you expect, then that's what you will see." ~ Lu

"I think that they look like whatever we think is beautiful and inspiring – from people to animals to plants – to a lovely warm sunny day." ~ Mel

This quote from Brenda may bring you comfort, too:

"I have been visited by my lost loved ones in dreams and they look better, healthier and happier. They have a peaceful glow about them and look flawless."

When I asked my partner Bob how he sees Angels, he told me that he sees them as *"auras of colour, my Dad is a sunny yellow"* and my daughter Gemma says *"I've seen my Dad in the form of orbs of light surrounding and protecting Charlie."*

(Charlie is Gemma's son – my grandson).

My Aunty tells me that she sees just facial expressions – such as the grin my husband used to give her when he was up to mischief, or the smile my Uncle would have on his face if something "naughty" came onto the television!

A friend of mine, Tina, who is very intuitive, sees her Angels with increasing bands of light-filled colour on their wings. i.e: the longer they have been gone from this earthly plane, the more colours they develop surrounding the edges of their wings – roughly one for each decade – interesting!

I have personally been lucky enough – blessed even, to have seen a vision of Archangel Raphael at a time when I was quite unwell and asking him for help. He appeared as a large being, his aura was more of a 'yellowy' green than the emerald green we may all expect and he appeared to be leaning over me in my bed. I couldn't see his face, it was very vague, but felt him hold my hand, and then enfold me within his large wings, making me feel safe and helping me to heal – which I did over the following weeks.

Maria K describes Archangel Uriel as *"massive, tall and golden"* after seeing him standing in front of a large arched window, and here's what Kimberly W and Simone say about their Archangel visions:

"When practicing Reiki on a friend I saw Archangel Michael hovering up by the ceiling. He was so large that he filled the whole ceiling in the grand master suite of the house we were renting. His robes were the most vibrant blue I have ever seen and they were billowing and floating around him. He was beautiful." ~ *Kimberly W*

"When I was a little girl I recall seeing Archangels Michael and Raphael at the foot of my bed. Michael was very big, as tall as the ceiling and his clothing was covered in plates of armour. He held a staff with a blue crystal sphere on top and had an amazing blue aura around him. Raphael was not quite as big and wore flowing green robes, held a golden bowl and had a golden and green aura around him. When I asked what was in the bowl he said it was a healing balm, then I remember being worried & asking if I was sick or was going to get sick and

*he replied that no, it was for healing my soul.
Both had beautiful huge wings. Now I quite
often see blue orbs and sparkles and am
comforted to know Archangel Michael is still
with me." ~ Simone*

As with everything connected to the angelic
realm, however you see or perceive the
members of your own Angel team, or in fact the
Archangels, is very personal to you. There can
never be any right or wrong way of visualising
those who give you so much unconditional love,
comfort and protection as they always do.
Remember - believing is seeing!

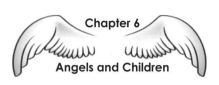

Chapter 6

Angels and Children

From when we are born we are naturally very open and receptive to things that we may unwittingly close our minds to as we grow up.

Children accept seeing their Angels on a regular basis and think that it's as normal as seeing you or I, so when they speak about them they should be encouraged to do so openly.

Many children have "imaginary friends" and it's my personal belief that these friends are from the angelic realms and visit children as protective and fun playmates.

When my daughter Gemma was a baby she would often look into one particular corner of the room, smiling and laughing at what appeared to be nothing at all. I always said that she was seeing my Nana who I believe to be her Guardian Angel but, of course, Gemma remembers nothing about it now!

I also have a picture of my son gazing up at the ceiling, taken when he was about 3 yrs old. After the picture was developed we saw two beams of light extending from his head as far as the eye could see – was he communicating with his Angels? I believe so.

My grandson, Charlie, tells us stories of his Grandad coming to see him and playfully bouncing with him on his bed, he also told his Mum on one occasion that Grandad was sitting in the garden with them whilst she was trying to put a new patio set together.

As Grandad was known as "Mr Fixit" when he was alive and she was having difficulty putting the parts together to start with, I can quite believe that this was one occasion he had definitely come to help her!

You may have heard of similar occurrences or experiences related by children, or even have children of your own who talk about their celestial playmates.

Here are a few of the experiences I have been told about:

"When my son was about 7 yrs old I left him playing on the computer in his room whilst I sorted laundry in mine. When I went to check on him a few minutes later and asked if he was okay, he barely looked up from the computer and said 'Oh, Mum …. Nanny Twiggybush has been.' (Nanny's surname was Twig)

When I prompted him further he said 'Yes, she came in and sat on my bed watching me. Then she asked if I had been a good boy'. He told me that she then smiled at him, got up from the bed and walked through the wall into my room." ~ Sharon

"When my grand-daughter was 6 yrs old, she told me there was a man in my living room stealing a rose, so I went to look but nobody was there.

She said 'Cant you see him Nana?' I didn't want to upset her by saying no, so I answered 'Yes I can but who can he be?' she then said 'He's told me he loves you, and he's your Grandad'.

She also told me that he was wearing very funny clothes and a flat cap and had a beautiful smile

57

– a perfect description of my Grandad who had passed over 28 years before. This was two years ago and I'm proud and happy to say that she has seen him many times since." ~ Moira

"When my Nan passed recently, my daughter told me that she was now with Grandpa (my Grandad) and he was now going to show her around and they were going to have a big party to celebrate her going home!" ~ Catherine

"My nephew Aiden often talks about his great Grandad who passed when Aiden was a baby and says his Grandad looks after him.
On one occasion his Mum found him in the process of climbing over the stair safety gate but was unable to get to him as quickly as she wanted to. She was sure he was about to fall right down the stairs. However, it seemed that something suddenly stopped him from doing so and he regained his balance. He told his Mum she shouldn't worry as his Grandad had saved him from falling!" ~ Josie

"My son doesn't remember any of this now but when he was 6/7 years old he used to tell me about an Angel, a tiny one that would sit on top of his wardrobe and talk to him as he went to sleep. When I put tinsel on top of his wardrobe that Christmas, he even insisted that I had to leave a space for where the Angel would sit! He said that Angels looked like normal people but had wings and could fly, and that everybody had an Angel with them and he could see them all. He even drew a picture of mine and called her Mary - it's a picture I have kept to this day.

He also went on holiday around that time with my sister and her family. Her husband, Simon had undergone a heart bypass operation earlier that year and my son told me he saw Simon's Angel too, and it was the biggest Angel he had ever seen!" ~ Sarah

"I caught my two boys laughing and talking away with their Grandad (who passed away 4 yrs ago). When I asked them what was happening they told me that he had asked them if he could have one of their sweeties, so they were sharing them with him! It was amazing" ~ Margaret

As you can see from all of the above stories, children have the most amazing natural perception and visions of Angels – wouldn't it be wonderful if we all kept that same wonderful ability right through into adulthood?

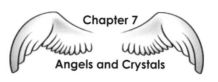

Chapter 7

Angels and Crystals

Crystals are extraordinary things and have histories and secrets which sometimes go back for thousands of years.

I first became attracted to them in 2003 when I visited my local crystal shop. As soon as I walked in there I felt incredibly peaceful and safe. A wonderful girl, Tora, spoke with me for some time to work out which crystal could help me the most and we decided on Smoky Quartz, an excellent stone for those who are grieving and fearful as I was at that time.

I bought a small piece, shaped like a pebble because it felt 'just right' when I held it. At home later that day I held the crystal up to the window to look at it in the light. On doing so I could very clearly see the word "LOVE" written inside it. I immediately knew that it was a message from my late husband letting me know that he was there to support me.

I kept that crystal with me at all times over the following months and it now has a special place in a little Angel trinket box with a couple of other small reminders of how my Angel team helped me to get through that terrible period in my life.

Since then my crystal collection has grown enormously and I have them all over the house. You are probably aware that there are many you can choose from to help with healing on all levels, but did you know that there are crystals which will help you connect to the angelic realms?

My favourite for this purpose is **Celestite.** I keep a beautiful cluster of it with my Angel cards at all times and place it on my lap whilst I am carrying out my readings. I find it an excellent aid to angelic communication.

I also have a large piece of **Apophyllite** which I keep on my desk – my personal choice for creating an extra connection to the spiritual realm. It is also known for enhancing intuition, so is a valuable extra aid to the work I do.

Other crystals known for aiding connection to the angelic forces are:

Angelite – This is a compressed form of celestite. Its shape often resembles a pair of Angel's wings which, of course, makes it a very popular choice for those who work with the celestial realms.

Selenite – is a beautiful and pure white stone which is said to amplify spiritual contact, particularly when used in angelic meditation.

Muscovite, **Danburite** and **Morganite** are all also said to be useful for angelic contact too, although I have no personal experience of working with them.

If you are looking for a crystal to help you to connect with your Angels on a celestial level, the best thing you can do is to visit a crystal shop and ask if you can hold the various stones listed above and see what feels right for you. Trust me – you'll know when you find it, the crystal you need will always find its way to you!

As well as creating a universal connection to the angelic realms you may also wish to carry the crystal that resonates with the energies of the various Archangels.

Each Archangel has their own crystal affinities – both those that harmonise with the colour of their auras and those which aid you with their areas of "expertise" – the reason you may be calling on them. Crystal tumble stones are usually very reasonably priced, so you could choose to carry both if you wish.

The following list tells you which crystals are associated with our Archangels auras and what issues the stones could help you with, too.

The first crystal listed beneath each Angel's name will be the one that matches their aura colour. You will then see at least one aspect of each Archangel's expertise and the stone associated with helping you with the same.

Archangel Ariel
Aura affinity: Rose Quartz
Prosperity: Citrine

Archangel Azrael
Aura affinity: Yellow Calcite
Grieving: Smoky Quartz
Aiding restful sleep: Amethyst

Archangel Chamuel
Aura affinity: Fluorite
Love: Rose Quartz
Confidence: Citrine

Archangel Gabriel
Aura affinity: Citrine
Creativity: Citrine
Fertility: Moonstone

Archangel Haniel
Aura affinity: Moonstone
Energy/Vitality: Topaz

Archangel Jeremial
Aura affinity: Amethyst
Problem solving: Green Tourmaline

Archangel Jophiel
Aura affinity: Pink Tourmaline
Attracting Joy: Topaz

Archangel Metatron
Aura affinity: Watermelon Tourmaline
Motivation: Carnelian

Archangel Michael
Aura affinity: Sugalite
Protection: Clear Quartz or Amber

Archangel Raguel
Aura affinity: Aquamarine
Sorting out feelings: Blue Lace Agate

Archangel Raphael
Aura affinity: Malachite
Healing: Malachite or Jade

Archangel Raziel
Aura affinity: Clear Quartz
Clairvoyance: Apophyllite or Lapis lazuli

Archangel Sandalphon
Aura affinity: Turquoise
Tranquillity: Chrysoprase

Archangel Uriel
Aura affinity: Amber
Inspiration: Chrysolite

Archangel Zadkiel
Aura affinity: Lapis Lazuli
Clarity: Peridot

Chapter 8

Discovering your Guardian Angel

Your Guardian Angel is assigned to you at birth and remains with you throughout your life. We all call upon our Guardian Angel for help at times, although we don't always know their names. Wouldn't it be nice to find out?

Try this way of discovering your Guardian Angel's name:

1. Take yourself off somewhere quiet where you won't be disturbed – this could be into a room indoors or out into nature if you prefer.

2. Make your space as relaxing as possible, in whatever way works for you. You could light a candle, burn an incense stick or play music (no lyrics) if you wish.

3. Relax your body completely and empty your mind of all negative thoughts and emotions.

4. Concentrate on your breathing to ensure complete relaxation. (You could try the "square breathing" exercise here that my Reiki Master, Jason, taught me – breathe in for the count of 4, hold for the count of 4, breathe out for the count of 4, hold for the count of 4 and so on …).

5. Focus on your own full birth name and birth date.

6. Now ask "Guardian Angel of mine – please reveal your name to me" having the faith that you will receive an answer.

7. Listen for a name to present itself to you, it may not be audible but it will become strong and prominent in your mind – remember that a lot of Angelic names are unusual or strange to pronounce so don't be surprised if it is a name you haven't heard of!

Now, after thanking them for revealing their name to you, write down the name of your Guardian Angel, fold the paper up and place it in a place that is special to you – you may have a small Angel altar, or box – or you may have a crystal or other treasure you would like to keep with it – remember that anywhere that feels right for you to keep the name IS right.

When you next feel the need to call on your Guardian Angel you will then be able to do so by their given name – you can use the following prayer if you wish to do so.

"My Guardian Angel (*say the name of your Guardian Angel here) **I call upon you, and thank you for loving me through all that I do, Please shield and protect me and show me the way, and carry me through to the end of each day"**

Chapter 9

Angel Prayers, Poems and Blessings

I've written many Angel blessings, poems and prayers over the years and have selected some of my favourites for inclusion in this book. I hope they give you comfort and inspiration when you are in need and that you will pass them on to friends and relatives who may enjoy them, too.

~ Archangel Prayers ~
These prayers are short and simple in order that they may be easily recalled.

~ *The Healing Prayer* ~
"Sweet Raphael, I call on you,
I know that you are there,
and ask you for your healing strength
in answer to my prayer.
Please take away the sadness,
take away the pain,
hold me in your healing wings
and make me whole again"

~ *The Prayer for restful sleep* ~
"Dear Azrael, I call on you to
help me sleep tonight,
with peace and calm the whole night through
until the morning light.
Please send me sweet and restful dreams to
calm and still my mind,
so that I may sleep the night away, leaving all
my worries behind."

~ The Prayer for true love ~
Dear Chamuel I'm asking for
your help from above
to unite me with my Soulmate –
twin hearts so full of love.
I promise to treasure this blessing you send –
my Soulmate, my lover, a rock, my best friend.

~ The Prayer for protection ~
"I call on you, dear Michael
to protect me through all I do,
empowering me with courage
and the strength to see me through."

~ Angel Blessings ~
A collection of blessings to bestow upon those
you love.

~ Blessing for a new week ~
A brand new week, a bright new day,
May your Angels guide you
every step of the way,
bring you love and happiness,
keep your life calm
and most of all protect you from harm.

~ Daily Blessing ~
May all your troubles be tiny
and all your worries small
and your Angels come and smooth your way
whenever you may call.

~ Bed-time Blessing ~
May your Angels visit you whilst you sleep
and bless you with beautiful dreams to keep.

~ Bed-time Blessing 2 ~
Imagine yourself sleeping in your Angel's wings,
then dream amid the peace
that thought will bring.

~ Soulmate Blessing ~
May your love life blossom
and your dreams come true,
by your Angels bringing your Soulmate to you.

~ Friendship Blessing ~
"Here is my wish-list for my friends,
to bring them contentment before the day ends
A pinch of faith and a cupful of hope,
a handful of courage to help them cope,
an abundance of health and a heart full of love,
all brought down to them
from their Angels above"

~ Healing Blessing ~
May you feel the comfort of your Angel's wings,
and be blessed with the
healing that they can bring.

~ Blessing for a new life ~
May the Angels bless this baby,
so perfect and pure,
and protect, love and guide him
through all of life's doors.
May he have good health and happiness
and a life full of love,
being watched over always
by his Angels above.

~ Angel Poems ~

~ Trust your Angels ~

If you're feeling low or lonely just
call your Angels near,
and ask them for their guidance
to free you from your fears.
They'll always give you comfort
and send something from above
to help you find contentment
through their unconditional love.
It may well be that what they send
is not what you expect,
but you'll see with time and hindsight
it was for your very best!

~ There's always an Angel ~

Monday's Angel looks down from above,
Tuesday's Angel will wrap you in love,
Wednesday's Angel is healing and caring,
Thursday's Angel shares the
load you are bearing,
Friday's Angel will shoulder your woes,
Saturday's Angel will lift you, when low,
Sunday's Angel will send you affection,
and steer you and point you
in your life's direction.
All of your Angels are protective and giving
you reason to cherish the life you are living.
Whenever you need them, whatever the day,
your Angels will be there to show you the way.

*(Inspired by "Monday's Child" the famous early
19th century rhyme)*

~ Signs ~

"The sparkle of light, the whisper of wings
the fleeting touch that an Angel can bring,
will bring you guidance and
surround you with love,
with the comforting presence that
comes from above.
A feather, a coin or a butterfly in view,
can also be signs you have Angels with you.
Acknowledge their presence, trust in their care,
and thank them for showing you that they are
there."

~ My Angel Star ~
(for Luke)
Twinkle, twinkle little star,
are you who I think you are?
Up above my world you fly,
watching me as night goes by,
I feel you close, though you're afar,
twinkling bright - my Angel Star.

*(Inspired by the well known 19th century rhyme
published by Jane Taylor, 1806)*

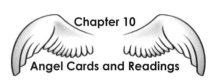

Chapter 10

Angel Cards and Readings

What are Angel Cards and how can they help us?

Angel Cards are very gentle, designed with the intention of imparting comfort and reassurance to the recipient of a reading.

I have never come across a deck of Angel Cards which have had a single message that could scare anyone who uses them (as tarot cards sometimes can). My own deck of cards, "A Pocketful of Angels" created in 2010, hold only messages of encouragement and reassuring guidance.

The angelic messages we receive through the cards can steer us towards the happiness and peace of mind that we all hope to achieve in our lives. This guidance is given through the messages contained in the chosen cards which are drawn by the reader using angelically inspired instinct.

Most people who own a deck of Angel Cards just like to draw their own personal cards to gain daily or weekly insight into their own lives, gaining considerable guidance from doing so. Then there are other people – like myself - who read the cards regularly for others, too.

Angel Card Readings can be amazingly accurate and give us comforting guidance when we need it the most.

I believe that we all have it within us to be able to read the cards - all we have to do is believe in ourselves and our ability to communicate with our Angels.

Remember too, that your Angel team will be there standing by and waiting to help you.

To simplify things if you are doing a reading for someone else, visualise your Angel team connecting to theirs. Between them you will get all the guidance you need!

If you would like to tap into your own abilities and do Angel Card Readings yourself, simply follow the steps below.

Selecting your Angel Card Deck

Choose a deck which you are naturally drawn to - which ones do your instincts tell you are right for you? There are numerous decks available by various Angel Card Authors, and they can be bought from bookshops, new age/spiritual shops - also by mail order on-line.

Some decks have the full Angelic messages on the cards, others have a short message and a guide book which expands on the full meaning. If buying from a local shop ask the owner if they have open decks that you can look at and get a feel for. If purchasing on line see if there are images of samples of some of the cards - also testimonials from those who have purchased the cards already. Any good on-line outlet will have a contact form in order that you can ask questions if you want to.

Getting to know and attuning to your Angel Cards.

Some Angel Card decks come with a guide book including instructions on how to approach this - my own Cards come with an "Attuning to and working with your Angel Cards" document. Most of the following wording is taken from there and can apply to any set of cards that you may have purchased, so please follow the steps below:

Step 1. Take a quiet moment by yourself to open your cards.
Step 2. Hold the cards to your heart and ask your Angels to bless them and to help you to read the cards accurately.
Step 3. Now go through the cards, touching every one in turn to infuse them with your energy.
Step 4. "Play" with the cards – read them, shuffle them, fan them out, spread them out on a table or on the floor – whatever you feel that you want to do.

All of these actions energise the cards and tune them in to your own vibrations – familiarising yourself in this way will enable you to connect to the cards with both your conscious and sub-conscious self.

Carrying out your Readings
* Still your mind, hold the cards to your heart and ask the Angels to communicate clearly through the cards.
* When doing a Reading for yourself, simply ask your Angels to either answer your given question or to just tell you that which they want you to know by guiding you to choose the relevant cards.
* When doing a Reading for someone else, dedicate the cards to whomever you are doing the Reading for.

You will most likely find your own words, but you could try something simple such as *"I dedicate these cards to ******* (here you can also give their date of birth, location and any other details that you want to), please, Angels, help me to give them a true and accurate reading that will help and guide them in the best possible way that we can"*. You can say this silently to yourself if you wish.

* Shuffle the Angel Cards until you feel guided to stop and then choose the first card that your instinct takes you to. You may like to choose just one card or continue to do a three card spread in the same way.

Whatever feels right for you will be absolutely right with your Angels.

* Study the messages on each card. Please trust your intuition when reading your messages, your first instincts will invariably be right when interpreting how the message relates to you and your current circumstances. If the Reading is for someone else, ask them to do the same - trust *their* instincts when interpreting the messages you are passing to them.

Helpful tips:
* Always do the readings in a quiet room or place, away from any other distractions.
 * Sometimes a card will fly from the pack whilst you shuffle, or simply stick out. Always pay extra attention to these cards as they could be important messages from the Angels.
* Have faith in your ability to choose the right card(s) when doing a Reading. If it helps, remind

yourself that your Angels are your guiding hand and that they are ultimately the ones who are choosing the cards for you.

* Remember that often the messages from the Angels contained in a reading will have immediate relevance, but sometimes it may be up to several weeks before you or the person you have read for will think back to the reading and realise what it was that the Angels were trying to communicate.

* Always remember to say "thank-you" to your Angels after every Reading.

* Whilst you are not using or carrying your cards with you, store them in a light and airy place with, or surrounded by crystals, Angel figures or something else that is special to you – you will instinctively know where and how you want to keep them because again, you will be guided by your Angels.

* The most important thing is that you get pleasure from using your cards – enjoy!

Chapter 11

True Angel Encounters

I have dedicated this entire chapter to Angel stories and encounters that I have received from other people, with just one at the end from myself.

I've received many stories over recent months and have chosen those that I feel are the most moving or inspiring to pass on to you.

I have no reason to doubt that these are completely true accounts of genuine events and have been given permission from all of the writers to publish them here, allowing us all to share their incredible experiences.

~ Daniel's Miracle ~
by Sharon May Sauboorah

My son Daniel was 12 years old and attended Bishops' Stopford School in Enfield.

The bell rang, announcing the end of the last class. Suddenly the halls and corridors became full with youngsters, as they came flooding out of the classrooms. Daniel was on the top floor in the West Wing and just like all the others, he was eager to get to registration. They wanted to sign in for the last time of the day and escape the restraints of school.

Daniel went to wait for his best friend by the stairs. They were in the same registration class, so they usually waited for each other. This was when the accident happened; this was when my son fell 3 floors. Whilst waiting, Daniel stupidly sat on the railing surrounding the stairwell. A young lad shoved into Daniel and this caused my son to lose his balance. The next moment he was falling straight through the middle of the stairwell and down onto the concrete floor below.

Now I can't relay anything else about the accident, all I can do is to tell the story from the time I arrived. The funny thing is, usually my son would walk home with his siblings and friends. This particular day, I decided to go to collect them and drive them home. A voice inside me told me to go to the school, that something was wrong.

Upon arriving at the school, friends of my children were shouting out to me. They were all crying and upset. It was hard for me to comprehend or indeed understand just what had happened. After all, my kids were in school and you always assume that they are safe. You never expect anything to happen to them.

I remember quickly parking in the school car park and one of the girls running in front to guide me to where my son was laying, flat on his back. There was no movement; his body was motionless and still. This was every parent's nightmare.

All I wanted to do was to rush to his side; my boy needed me. The head teacher tried to keep me at bay but I brushed her aside. As quick as I could I knelt down beside my son and called his name. I held his hand and pushed his fringe back off of his face. The tears ran down my face, whilst my heart beat so hard I thought it would erupt from my chest. The head teacher told me he had fallen from the top floor onto his back. This made me look up and stare. It was so far up and there was nothing to break his fall.

All I could do was to pray for God and the Angels to please, help my son. Don't take him away from me.

The ambulance arrived and the paramedics came to my son. Within minutes, they had checked his vital signs, put a brace on him, placed him carefully onto a board then moved him into the ambulance. There was no way I was leaving his side, so I climbed into the ambulance and sat next to him. He was still unconscious but he was breathing. The paramedic told me to keep talking to Daniel as this might stimulate a response. Thank God, my son heard my voice and he moved his eyelids. He mumbled 'Mum', I was so grateful to hear him say that word. Mum, sorry…. he kept muttering these words over and over again. This was a good sign; maybe God had heard me, maybe.

With the siren blaring, the ambulance arrived quickly at the hospital. The whole of A&E had come to a standstill. The ambulance doors were flung open and my son was rushed into the emergency resuscitation room. I could only stand back in horror as at least 9 doctors and nurses worked on my son. His clothes were cut away from his body. I remember watching his favourite coat being cut into shreds and thrown onto the floor. His shoes were dropped onto the floor; even his socks were removed.

A nurse took my hand and led me into the corridor. She explained that they needed to do tests and that it would be best for me to wait outside. I wanted to be with my son but she explained that the top consultants had all been called. These specialists were there to tend to my boy. They had all dropped what they were doing to rush to my Daniel. These consultants were specialists in brain damage, spinal damage, internal bleeding, organ damage etc…Again I prayed, I prayed as hard as I could. It seemed to take an eternity, but eventually the main consultant came over to speak to me. My husband had now arrived, so we stood side by side to face the worst. With tears running down my face, I asked 'is my son okay, please, what's wrong with my boy?'. My husband and I gripped each other's hand tightly.

The Doctor looked at me, then took my other hand in his and spoke "Your son is fine; there is nothing wrong with him".

I felt confused and asked him "How is this possible, are you sure?"

He shook his head and said, "We have done every test on him, including an MRI scan. He doesn't even have a bruise".

Everything seemed surreal; I caught my breath and asked him how this was possible. I had seen the height that he had fallen from.

He replied, "Sometimes we come across what we call 'A Medical Miracle', we don't know how it happens, we have no explanations. Your son is a Miracle".

Within minutes I was holding my sons hand and stroking his face. He looked so pale but he was alive, he was healthy. How had he managed to come out of this unscathed though, how? I decided to ask him if he could remember what had happened.

This is what he told me: He remembered falling and being very frightened. The next thing was the feeling of arms around him, of someone holding him tightly. He landed on his back but said it was as if he had been placed onto a pillow, and then it was as if he had gone into a deep sleep. The first thing he remembered waking up, was hearing my voice.

Now to most of you this story seems hard to believe but it is true and witnessed by many. Maybe some of you will try to rationalise it but for me...It was the day the Angels saved my son ...It was Daniel's Miracle.

~ My Baby's Guardian Angel ~
by Kara Mann

One day when my daughter, who is now 6, was only 11 months old, we were heading to Dublin for the day for a spot of Christmas shopping. We live in Wexford which is about a 2 hour drive from Dublin.

As usual, before a long drive, I had checked the oil, tyres and water on the car and topped up the water tank for the windscreen washers. When all was in order we set off in the car and put on my daughters favourite nursery rhyme CD.

After about 15 minutes she was asleep. Then 20 minutes into the journey the windscreen became dusty and dirty (because we were travelling behind a truck), so my husband switched on the windscreen washer. It didn't work. He tried again and again but still no water. Thinking that I had maybe put the water into the wrong part of the engine, he said that he would pull over so that he could check.

He stopped the car and as the cd switched off we both heard a horrible sound coming from the back of the car. Our precious little daughter was choking on her own vomit. I ran around and opened her door and sat her forward in her car seat. She let out the biggest cry and started breathing normally again.

We calmed her down, cleaned her up and re-started the car to head back home, but in all the panic we'd forgotten all about finding out why the windscreen washer wasn't working before going back onto the road.

After my husband started the car, he automatically switched on the windscreen washer to clear the dirty screen. It worked instantly! We both just looked at each other in amazement.

I honestly believe that an Angel gave us the warning to pull over that day. If the washer had been working then we would not have pulled over and therefore wouldn't have heard our daughter choking.

Everyday I thank the Angels - I know she has one sitting on her shoulder.

~ A True Angel ~
by Lupe Rodriguez-Smith

This is a story my mom told me years ago - It involved a trip her and my dad went on, with us kids when we were very young. The car broke down whilst we were out in a very deserted area.

A farmer on a tractor stopped by and asked if my parents needed some help. He then towed the car to a nearby gas station where he worked on the car, and also fixed us sandwiches.

My dad thanked the man, and we went on our way. The next day my dad went back to the gas station to thank the man again, but he couldn't find it so he asked someone for directions. The man he asked told him he didn't know of any gas station in that area that was open, but there had been one in the area many years ago.

My dad went by and checked the area where that had been, and there was nothing there. They had encountered a true angel for sure!

~ Angel Feathers ~
by Stephanie Jones

Going back to the end of 2003, I had started to read some spiritual development books in the hope I would be able to make contact with my spirit guide. I started to find little white feathers in my home. I didn't know where they had come from; I didn't have anything in the house that contained feathers so I just sucked them up the vacuum cleaner and carried on with the housework.

Then I started to see little white feathers floating down in front of me when I was out walking my children to school. I just assumed that they had fallen off of a passing bird, but when I looked up there were never any birds to be seen. I started watching a programme on Living T.V. called Psychic Live. A lady on the programme spoke about Angels and how they left white feathers as a sign to show they were around.

The next time I saw a white feather float down in front of me I said in my head "Okay, Angels if that is you sending these white feathers, can you please leave one somewhere I wouldn't expect to find one!" I was walking my son home from school and he had run on ahead.

When I got to the front door he was sat on the doorstep waiting, next to him was a lovely white fluffy feather! I've since gone on to learn more about Angels and have had many other Angel

84

Experiences but that first one will always be so very special to me.

~ Archangel Healing ~
by Maria K

My daughter Jade, was in a lot of pain with a bad back and I was worried about her, fearing that she may have slipped a disc. I asked Archangel Michael to stand by her for strength and called upon Archangel Raphael asking that he heal her and free her from pain. I later had a vision where we were all in a dim underground operating room and I saw Archangel Raphael's hand going through Jade's back. It looked almost as if he was re-arranging something inside her; this lasted for at least 5 minutes. After that wonderful vision I asked for a further sign that all would be well. Two days later when I was driving to work a car pulled up beside me. The number plate was green and white and the lettering on the plate was "JADE". I thought the number plate to be very significant because of the colours also, as Jade's surname is White and I believed that the green represented Archangel Raphael's healing energy. I knew then that everything would be okay. Jade then recovered very quickly and was able to return to work within the week. Thank you Archangel Raphael!

~ Angels all around us ~
by David Roethler

Eight years ago I became very ill and was rushed into hospital to have emergency surgery on my colon and stomach. The Doctor had expected some improvement by the following morning but at around 4a.m. that morning I took a severe turn for the worse.

I remember that my pain seemed to disappear and as I looked towards the door it appeared to be glowing. Standing in the doorway I could see my father and grandmother who had both passed away some years earlier. They came to my bedside and my Dad told me that they had come to take me home. They stayed and chatted with me for several hours, asking me many questions about my wife and children and how I liked being married – just general chat and a lot of questions about my family.

Both my wife and the nurse told me afterwards that they could see my eyes appearing to follow something around the room, also that they could hear every word I said. My wife truly feared she was about to become a widow.

After a few hours my father and grandmother started to head for the door and I asked them where they were going, as I thought they had come to take me home? My father turned to me and said that it wasn't my time to go yet after all as I still had work to do. He told me that I was in for a rough time but not to worry as he would be with me throughout, and that they both would still be there waiting for me when my time to go was due in the future.

86

I had to have several more operations but in time did make a full recovery and now have a completely different outlook on life because of my experience. I know that one day I will be re-united with my father and grandmother and until then I feel safe in the knowledge that our Angels really are all around us looking after us every day.

~ Angel Babies ~
by Lu Brennan

I have strayed off my spiritual path many times in my life and had done so again during the last year when life events such as the birth of my sixth child and moving home took precedence. This is the story about how my Angel babies steered me back onto my path. For many years I had been looking for some music to play in the background for when I do my healing work. It had always been disappointing as CD after CD just didn't have what I was looking for.

A few months ago I decided to shut down my regular Facebook page and open a new one.

I just felt so strongly that I needed to do this. Within 2 days I got a friend request from someone in Australia. I don't normally accept requests from people I don't know but something told me to do so. I felt at ease with it. It turned out that he had lived just down the road from where I live now, although I had never met him, and that he had written his own music that was a little different. He gave me a link to download a few tracks from his site.

When I went onto the site there was a background page of a cloudy sky and in the centre of the page was a rectangular box that flashed from image to image. They were moving quite slowly and as they switched I caught a glimpse of an image in the clouds. As I squinted to see more clearly the flashes slowed right down until I saw that the image I could see in the clouds was of an Angel baby girl.

I noticed it looked quite like my own children, but didn't think for one second it was a sign of anything bad. I went away from the page for a while and when I went back later it was still there. In fact, I could see the whole picture in the clouds and wow, more Angel Babies, both boys and girls. I instantly knew they were my lost babies (I've had quite a few) and that they had come to let me know the time was right for me to get firmly back onto my spiritual path.

It has to be the single most amazing experience of my life to date and I will never forget it. I am now a member of a circle where we have been connecting with Spirit and Angels and I have since become much more aware when reading Angel Cards. And yes, the music that I went to the site to listen to was exactly what I have spent the last 6 years and many euro searching for!

Thank you Angels and of course my Angel babies.

~ Nana's Angels ~
by Vicki Flynn

When I was 9 yrs old my Dad's mother passed away from cancer on his birthday. It was only the second time I had ever seen my Dad cry. My heart was broken at the loss of my Nana and broken twice over for my Dad's loss too.

He wanted to be left alone to grieve, so my Mom, sister, one of my brothers and I all went off into my Mum and Dad's bedroom together. I was sitting on the dresser facing the bed which had a huge wooden headboard.

My Mum was doing her best to comfort us and one of the things she said was "Remember, children, there are Angels all around us".

As she said that I looked up and towards the bed. Directly above the headboard were two Angels, one blonde and one brunette. Both were wearing long thick robes with thick golden belts, and they were wearing golden sandals too. It was as if time had stopped. They both smiled at me and I smiled right back at them.

I knew then that my Nana was safely with the Angels and that we would all be okay, too.

~ Saved by Angels ~
by Maurice Voice

After a relaxing three day break in Glastonbury, my wife, our two friends and I packed away our camping equipment and set off towards the motorway for the long journey home to Liverpool. The journey north takes us up the M5

Motorway to Birmingham where we change motorways and join the M6. It was this part of the journey that provided proof of what I always believed. On the M6 northbound the inside lane was full of slow moving traffic with lots of orange flashing lights. We were passing this at 60MPH, when suddenly one of the vehicles pulled out of the inside lane straight into our path. All I could do was to brake as hard as I could and my car skidded and spun around. As the car was spinning everything went into slow motion and coloured light filled the car. I was able to look around and everyone in the car was being held and protected in their seats by beings made of what I believe to be pure light. The car finally came to a halt on the central reservation facing the opposite way and the car was a complete write off. Four of us were in the car that day and the only injury suffered was caused by a seatbelt pre-tensioner!

I already had a strong belief in Angels and was sure I had someone watching over me when I was very young. This experience completely confirmed that which I always knew – that our Angels are always with us and like to look after us – All four of us believe that the Angels saved our lives that day.

~My Miracle Child~
by Jamir

Following two difficult pregnancies I was regretfully sterilised for medical reasons as the doctors thought my body could not possibly endure a third. Four years later my youngest son Jarek was born. This was only the first miracle surrounding his life, my story here is about the second.

Jarek was a sickly baby, suffering from countless allergies and terrible eczema. When he was just 18 months old he fell into my friend's pool. I rushed into the pool and dragged his poor little floating body out but he wasn't breathing, and he was blue with blood spots all under his skin from lack of oxygen. It was the middle of winter so the cold alone would have been enough to shut down his organs. I was terrified.

While my friend left me alone with him to phone for the ambulance, I desperately did some mouth to mouth resuscitation and whilst doing so I just knew that I wasn't alone with him and that Jarek was being protected. Whisps of wind kept brushing my tears and drying my face and I kept hearing a voice saying "just believe and all will be well".

By the time the ambulance arrived, I had Jarek breathing but he was comatose, so they took him in the ambulance to the nearest hospital which was 3/4 hr away. I rushed off in my car after him with this breeze still surrounding my face.

At the hospital, after they had done initial treatment and tests, they told me it was now just a waiting game, to see if he would ever wake up, but they warned me that there appeared to be no sign of brain activity.

I sat by his bedside holding his tiny little hand and just waiting, believing, knowing everything would be alright but not being able to get anyone else to understand. I talked with his

Angel the whole time and I was assured again that he would be fine as he had special work to complete. After about 14 hours Jarek opened his eyes and asked me for something to eat - no one could believe the miracle before our eyes except me!

I was allowed to take him home the next day as the doctors could see no reason to keep him in – in fact he was running around the hospital ward so boisterously, I think they were glad to see us go! Once home he wanted cheese – one of the things he had always been allergic to and after trying a little I found that he had no reaction to it at all. I gradually realised that all of his allergies had disappeared, along with his eczema and he has not had any sign of either since that awful day!

At this time a distinctive perfect white spot of hair appeared on the back left side of his head which he still has to this day. Touched by an Angel? Definitely!

~ Canine Comfort ~
By Janet Mullinex

I was feeling very low because of problems at home and decided to go and sit in the park for a while, just to get away from everything.

I was chatting on my mobile phone with a very good friend when I noticed that someone was coming into the park with about twelve dogs. I guessed that with so many dogs, they must have been a dog walker.

As they walked past me, one of the dogs stopped and came over to where I was sitting, then just sat down right beside me and wouldn't budge. I said "hello little doggy, what's your name?", then noticed that he had a collar with a disc on it so bent down to have a look. His name was "Angel".

The dog walker waited patiently for him but he didn't seem to want to leave me, so eventually she had to come over and coax him to re-join the other dogs.

My new friend definitely brightened my day and I'm sure that he was an Angel in doggy form sent to comfort me when I was in need. I will never forget him.

~ Divine Intervention ~
by Janette Harman

When I was 6 years old I was sent home from school very sick. Unfortunately my parents sent me back to school the next day only for me to be sent home again. My mother took me to the Doctor finally a day or so later and the Doctor told my parents not even to wait for an ambulance - to drive me immediately to the hospital themselves.

I remember lying on the back seat of the car feeling very strange and then the car filled with beautiful warm light. A man sat next to me on the seat and told me his name was Michael and he and his friend Raphael were going to help me and to not be scared. I felt so sleepy and warm, like I was enveloped in a massive gentle warm hug.

When I got to the hospital I was placed immediately on a bed (the doctor had phoned ahead and told them I was an emergency). The Doctor told my parents to give me a kiss as he wasn't sure what they could do for me but they would try their best. Again Michael came to me and repeated what he had said earlier. He told me he would not leave my side. I was raced straight to theatre and it turned out that my appendix had burst 2 days previously and were gangrenous. I should have died. When I woke up, Michael and Raphael were with me and to this day, have never left my side.

~ Answered Prayer ~
By Wendy Newsom

My Grand-daughter was in a coma in Great Ormond street hospital, she was 7 months old. In my despair I asked my Guardian Angel to visit her giving clear instructions on how to find her.

In the morning I travelled up from Brighton on the train to see her, this had been a daily thing for some time. When I arrived my daughter greeted me happily, saying that my grand-daughter had miraculously come out of her coma although no-body knew exactly why. What good news!

On my way home the train stopped at Tunbridge Wells and I decided to get off and wander up the street to a coffee bar. I felt a tickle on my ankle; a cotton thread was loose from my dress, so I bent down to tear it off. When I looked up again I saw a shop window in which a picture of an Angel holding a baby was prominent. When I asked the shopkeeper if I could please buy a copy of the poster he replied that he had no idea who had put it in the window and that there were no copies for sale.

I believe that my Guardian Angel had answered my prayers that day and wanted to be sure that I saw the Angel and baby poster as confirmation. Since that day I have believed more strongly in the power of good and always now speak with my Guardian Angel whenever I need their help.

~ Mind the bus ~
By Von Moss

Before I moved to Ireland I worked as a self employed gardener, this involved a lot of driving around the countryside in Wiltshire, England. At around about 7 a.m. on a Friday morning I was driving out to a client on a back road just outside a village called Uffington.

As I drove along I heard a soft voice talking to me – it seemed to be coming from the passenger seat area, although there was nobody else in the van.

This voice just said "*Mind the bus!*". For reasons I can never explain I slowed to a crawl as I rounded a sharp bend in the road and there coming straight towards me at high speed was a bus! Because I had almost stopped the bus driver just managed to avoid me.

As I drove on, a bit shaken up, I said "*Where did that voice come from?*" As I said this I heard the same voice I had heard before and it just said one word – "*Angel*".

~ Caught by an Angel ~
By Geraldine Burrows

I know for sure my Angels were behind me the day I was trying to get up the steps of the bus, with my baby David in the pram. I lost my balance as I climbed to enter the bus doors, and should have fallen backwards and landed on the ground. But, as I fell, I felt something was holding me upright and I found I was able to get safely onto the bus!

I was very shaken as I knew that if I had fallen backwards as I thought I was going to, that it may not have been just me that could have been badly injured as David could have fallen from the pram. I truly believe that I was caught by an Angel!

~ Grandad ~
By Christie Wordsworth

I have always been sure that my Grandad looks after my children and believed too that he may be my daughter's Guardian Angel as I was pregnant with her when he passed away.
My beliefs were confirmed on the day I decided to tidy my daughter's bedroom when she was 6 months old. She wasn't able to crawl at that stage so I sat her on the floor with a few toys around her. My son was 3 yrs old at the time and had suffered a twisted ankle and couldn't walk at all, so I sat him on the bed.
I climbed over a large set of drawers to pull some clothes from behind them. Suddenly the

chest of drawers tipped forward. I tried to grab them but as they were so large and heavy my fingers were slipping off them. I knew if I let go they would drop on my daughter and could cause her serious injury.

I called to my son "Jodice, please move your sister, quickly!". He was crying as he said "but Mam, I can't move because my ankle hurts", but he then managed to drop his bottom onto the floor and shuffled up to his sister. He couldn't manage to move her so he put his body over hers to protect her. The memory of that moment still makes me cry today.

I was panicking by now for the safety of both of my children and I looked to the window and shouted "Please help us!"

The next thing I knew was that I felt I could let go of the chest of drawers long enough to get to my children.

I climbed over from behind them, grabbed both of my kids and got them out of harm's way. All three of us were sobbing with relief.

When we had all calmed down after a few minutes, I looked at the chest of drawers and was amazed to see that they were still tilted forward. They had absolutely nothing to lean on; it was as if they were just tilted in mid air. I knew right then that Grandad, my daughter's Guardian Angel and protector of both my children had come to our aid and held the drawers for me so that I could get my children to safety.

A few months later, after an outing to take flowers to his grave, my daughter was waving up at the sky. When I asked her who she was waving at, she said "Grandad, Mummy – look, he's waving at me!". I am so happy that she can see her Guardian Angel!

~ Earth Angel ~
By Anna Sicova

I was feeling devastated by a relationship break up and was hurting so much that I couldn't stop myself from bursting into tears at a bus station. I felt terrible and that life was impossible, I couldn't stop crying.

Everyone who came near me quickly walked away until one lady came and sat down next to me. She passed me some bright white tissues and a bottle of water and just sat quietly listening to me pouring my heart out.

I suddenly felt a surge of love and everything seemed better somehow. I felt that I had been touched by an Angel. Whether this lady was an Angel, or had been sent by one, I don't know, but she has opened my heart to the spiritual world and I will never ever forget her.

~ Angelic Confirmation ~
By Danielle Rossetti

I recently had a massive decision to make. I had made the decision to separate from my husband and I had to move out and rent a house for myself and my 3 children. I found a great house but was feeling overwhelmed with the decision. I decided to consult my Angel Cards and chose the pack which has a 'yes' and 'no' card.

I was in tears at this point and asked for a clear answer. As I shuffled the 44 card pack, out flew a card across the room. The card was YES. I am so grateful and happy that I made that choice. Without the support of my Angels I'm not sure I would have made the big changes that I had to make.

~ 3 Deep ~
By Kim Rossignol

During a weekend retreat at my friend's camp, I had set up my massage table outside in a grove of trees. I called on Archangel Michael to surround the healing space and stand guard with his Band of Mercy while I did reiki on the ladies there. The camp is near her family home which we know to be inhabited by many spirits.

I called on Michael in order to keep the space clear as most of the time, crossed over loved ones come through to my clients, and I didn't want other spirits blocking those who may need to come through for my friends.

The sessions went beautifully with many communications. During a break in treatments I re-shielded our space, and mentally asked Michael how we were doing. As I sat with my eyes closed I heard him very clearly say, "We are 3 deep." When I scanned the area with my eyes closed, I saw very clearly what he meant. The first line was a circle of Angels including Archangel Michael, standing wing to wing, with quite literally a group of spirits peering into our circle, 3 deep!

At the end of the sessions I thanked Michael and his Band of Mercy for their protection. It is wonderful to know and have it confirmed, that when you call on the Angels, they are lovingly ready and anxious to help.

~ Don't worry ~
By Sondra Joyce

I was walking along the railroad tracks, taking the same shortcut home from my best friend's house where I had gone to visit a while after school, as we did quite often. It was getting close to graduation from Junior High school, in the ninth grade. It was customary to exchange graduation photos with ALL of your friends and acquaintances, so I had a billfold chocked so full of photos it would barely snap closed. I was 14 years old, plus.

Suddenly I stopped in my tracks and gasped, thinking "Oh no! Where is my billfold?" I looked in my purse and almost panicked. It wasn't there. I knew I hadn't dropped it on my walk home. I began to pray and pray "Oh, please dear God, let my billfold be at home". I kept repeating this over and over with tears running down my cheeks.

Suddenly, off to my right side, I heard this most kind, loving and angelic voice say, "Do not worry my child, it will be there". There is no doubt it was a male voice. To this day I am sure it was my Guardian Angel. All worry left me and I felt calm and happy again. I stepped up my pace to get home more quickly. Finally, in the side door and a dash to the dining room! There on the buffet lay my bulging red billfold.

I didn't tell anyone about this incident for a long time, I didn't even tell my best friend. Mostly because I thought they would think I was making it up, also because I felt strongly that it was a Holy experience, between me and God. Something not to be talked about casually. I feel to this day that this was a very blessed moment.

I am 75 years old now and in all the years since this happened, I have been able to remember the sound of that voice, just as though it happened yesterday. I feel strongly that when I pass, this Angel will be the one to help me.

His will be the first face I see.

~ The Healer's Miracle ~
by Nancy Walker

It was 12th March 1997 when I heard those terrible words 'I'm so sorry but you have leukaemia'. My mum collapsed next to me at my bedside at these words and I knew then, that I had a long, difficult, painful and extremely frightening journey ahead of me. However, I very quickly made up my mind that this disease was not going to beat me and that I would fight it every step of the way. I surrounded myself with cheerful things and played my favourite music to keep my spirits up.

The first two chemotherapy treatments were hard but I picked up quickly after them. Then in June, everything changed. I had just finished my third treatment and although it went well, I

101

contracted septicaemia and went into complete organ failure. The last thing that I remember before slipping away was no longer being able to breathe and my boyfriend asking me to marry him. I was in a coma for 5 days on a machine to help me breathe. A good friend of mine, a Catholic priest, even came to administer the last rites as I was not expected to last much longer.

The only thing I can remember about those 5 missing days of my life was being visited by the most beautiful being I had ever seen in my life. He stood magnificently tall, bathed in emerald green light and smiling. He had the most incredibly kind face and gloriously golden brown hair that shimmered. I felt utterly and completely loved and at peace. He told me that his name was Raphael which means 'God heals' and he told me that everything was going to be ok and that I would be granted a miracle because there was still important work for me to do.

He told me that I was healer just like him and that my life purpose was to bring healing to others. I knew that this was no dream... I knew that he spoke the truth and that I would make a complete recovery.

It is now 14 years later and I have been blessed with 4 wonderful children. I am still doing healing work and love every minute of it. Working with the Angelic Realm is simply incredible. If ever anybody had any doubts as to whether or not Angels truly exist.... point them in my direction. I am LIVING proof!"

~ Blessed by Angels ~
by Mary Jac

You will have read about some of my own angelic visions and experiences in earlier chapters. This story is my account of the celestial love and support I have been shown whilst writing and compiling this book and why I feel that it has been blessed by the Angels throughout …

I felt the "push" to start writing "Embracing our Angels" whilst on holiday in Looe, Cornwall. No surprise really as I have always thought of Looe as my spiritual home from the first time I visited there in the 1980's. From the moment I stepped out of the car there, over 30 years ago, I felt that I was "home" and have visited there as often as possible since. I have often wondered if I lived there in a previous lifetime. I can't think of a more perfect place for this book to have been 'born'.

From the moment I first started to gather my thoughts and ideas together for the book and put them onto paper I have been showered with countless signs of encouragement from my ever supportive team of Angels.

I've been blessed with white feathers appearing in front of me and white butterflies hovering beside me on an almost a daily basis. I've seen many feathers and Angels in the clouds and been visited by Angels in my dreams. I have also been sent a new pigeon friend who visits me regularly when I'm in the garden. My Animal Spirit Guide book tells me that a pigeon comes to tell you to "Keep your mind on the goal ahead, stay with it and you will get there" –

which is just what I have done to get this book completed!

I kept a record of some of the other signs of angelic support I was sent during this time so that I could share them here with you.

On the first morning following my decision to start the book I was on the beach in Looe quite early in the morning. The beach was very quiet and I was thinking about all the things I could share here with you, then decided to take a video with my phone to record the sight and sound of the waves to bring home with me. Whilst pointing my phone towards the shore I noticed that a white butterfly had come into my sight, it fluttered in front of me for a few seconds before settling on the sand a few feet away from me. I actually caught it on camera, thinking how unusual it was to see a butterfly on an open beach. I immediately took it as a sign of encouragement from the Angels - they liked the fact I had finally put pen to paper to write about them!

Throughout the week I was inspired with a whole host of ways in which I could convey the knowledge and experiences that I have been blessed with through the written word, so that I could share them with you, and wrote down thousands of words whenever we were relaxing on the beach or at the holiday flat. I felt that my Angels were with me, prompting me all the way.

On the last day of the holiday, we were again on the beach and I was sitting happily in the sunshine that we had been told not to expect, with a pad and pen on my lap.

I was wondering whether the writing would come as easily once I was home and back to the usual daily routine, when I had an urge to look up. I was really happy to see a cloud formation of several large white feathers above me – I think I was being told "Yes, it will!" – and it was!

On the way home we decided to break our journey in Glastonbury and I took several pictures in the beautiful and healing Chalice Well Gardens. I unknowingly took the image then which later showed the three Angels, which I have described in the "images within images" section in Chapter 3. It would seem that my Angels were standing near me that day and wanted me to physically see that they were there.

I continued with the writing when home, then a week or so later, whilst taking a break and having a family outing to Goodwood, I had no less than 4 celestial messages within as many hours! Firstly we had to pass the "Southgate" traffic turn off where we had to turn onto the A286 road. (Southgate was my Nana's maiden name and number 286 was where we lived with her when I was little). Whilst at Goodwood the third sign came in the form of a fluffy white feather on the grass right in front of me. The last sign came on the way home when we were stuck in traffic. I opened the car window as it was getting quite stuffy inside the car and a pretty red admiral was hovering beside me! Only that morning I had said to my partner Bob that we rarely see red admiral butterflies in our area like the one I had seen in Tintagel, Cornwall; in fact I hadn't seen one for years – until then!

The following day I found a second red admiral happily sunning himself in my fairy garden, wow, two in two days!

Over the next few weeks I had many more signs as mentioned above, then, on a night shortly before the completion of the book I went out into the garden. It was quite late, one of those really muggy nights where everything is totally still. It was very quiet and nothing was moving. I asked my Angels "What do you think? Do you like the book?".

As if in answer my wind chimes which hadn't moved for hours suddenly starting tinkling – just for a few moments. The breeze that seemed to come from nowhere to ring my chimes went away just as quickly. I'm sure that was the Angels' way of letting me know that they love everything in the book and that I have their blessing.

I'm so happy to know they approve as I couldn't have done it without them, and I'd like to thank them all for their help - my wonderful Angel team!

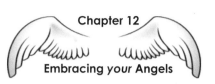

Chapter 12

Embracing *your* Angels

Throughout the time you have been reading this book, I'm sure that not only will you have been moved by some of the experiences here, but that you will have been inspired to further discover and embrace the Angels in your life.

Knowing that we are *never* alone and that we're surrounded by unconditional love and protection can bring us all enormous comfort and reassurance.

Angels will shine light onto our darkest days and will constantly find ways to show us how we can turn our lives around to find the happiness we all deserve.

I'll leave you here with a collection of quotes from friends telling us why they are so happy to embrace the Angels in *their* lives and why they think that everyone should do the same!

You should embrace your Angels because...

" ... *they are always there to help us when invited into our lives, all we have to do is ask*" ~ *Tracey*

" ... *they give unconditional love, and if you allow them, they will hold your hand too*" ~ *Francine*

" ... *they will change your life in a very special way helping you to step into your own power, and will lovingly ensure that you tap into all the beautiful gifts that are within you so that you may share them with the world." ~ Genevieve*

" ...Angels are Heaven's messengers and will always support, advise, guide, defend, protect, warn, heal, help and love us no matter whether we listen to them or not!" ~ Catriona

" ... they are lovingly and patiently awaiting our invitation to assist us and love to bring us guidance, support, joy and peace" ~ Kimberly

" ... they are always with us when we need them the most, bringing calm into our lives" ~ Lynette

" ... being open to help, guidance and love is a wonderful feeling" ~ Val

" ... when we fly with our Angels we can do anything our heart desires. With them we are pure unconditional love " ~ Betty

" ... they are there to protect and guide us on our life's journey! Who knows, they MIGHT be a relative or friend who has transitioned already" ~ Kenneth

" ... they will help you to find true inner peace" ~ Tania

" ... once you realise the Angels are with you, you see the real beauty that is all around you and material things just fade into insignificance. You realise you're never on your own, and that you're loved always" ~ Vera

" ...they will always help you in your hour of need. Angels never hurt us and will only love and guide us unconditionally. They only want the best for us and to protect us.

When I ask for help they show me the light in many colours to let me know they are with me, and I feel someone holding my hand at night until I fall asleep -

THATS ANGEL LOVE " ~ Moira

Acknowledgements

I have to thank Bob for his patience and endless cups of tea whilst I have been "away with the Angels" writing this book.

I also want to mention my daughter Gemma and her partner, Matt for their unfailing and unquestioning support over the past few years whilst I rediscovered myself through my strengthening awareness and connection to my Angels, and my lovely Grandson Charlie, just because he's gorgeous and brings me so much happiness!

Thank you too, to everyone who has happily contributed their stories here to help and inspire others, and special thanks of course, to my wonderful team of Angels!

About the Author

Mary Jac was born in Portsmouth, UK and has lived there for most of her life. She started to read Angel Cards for herself for comfort a few months after she was widowed in 2002, and then moved on to doing Readings for friends and family, soon realising how amazingly accurate they were. In 2008 she decided to do professional personal Angel Card Readings on line and has not looked back since – doing several readings every week through her own websites.

It was suggested to her some time ago that she should write her own set of Angel Cards, and in early summer 2010 felt that the time was right to do so – the titling and wording of "A Pocketful of Angels" came to her very easily, as did the creation of this book "Embracing our Angels" in the summer of 2011.

She says that she knows she has been helped through Angelic prompting – and thanks her Angels daily for all their help.

Mary has had an *Angel Expert* article published in 'Soul & Spirit' magazine, which has also given a very favourable review of her Angel Cards. Her website was also featured in 'Spirit & Destiny' magazine in early 2011.

She hopes that everybody gets as much pleasure and inspiration whilst using her cards and reading this book as she did whilst she was writing them, and that they both help bring Angelic inspiration and guidance to all who seek it through her work with the angelic realm.

Mary Jac's other work:

Mary's Angel Message Cards:
"A Pocketful of Angels"
Are available by mail order from the following
website:
www.pocketfulofangels.com
They are also for sale on Amazon and at
selected retail outlets.

Her main Angel website:
"My Angel Card Readings"
www.myangelcardreadings.com
Is a large and very popular site, attracting over
2000 visitors every day.
A beautiful site, it offers free on line Angel Cards
for you to choose from by your own angelically
guided instincts. You'll also find the Fairy Realm
and Unicorn World there!

The second, smaller 'sister' site
"Tranquil Waters"
www.tranquilwaters.uk.com
is also a very relaxing site
which you are sure to enjoy.

Mary also has pages on facebook which she
would love you to join, here:
www.facebook.com/maryjacangelcardreadings
www.facebook.com/pocketfulofangels

and you'll find her on Twitter, here:
www.twitter.com/AngelCardReader

You'll find the website for this book at:
http://www.embracingourangels.com